ON SUNNY DAYS WE SANG

A HOLOCAUST STORY
OF SURVIVAL AND RESILIENCE

JEANNETTE GRUNHAUS DE GELMAN

ap

ISBN: 9789493276208 (ebook)

ISBN: 9789493276185 (paperback)

ISBN: 9789493276192 (hardcover)

Publisher: Amsterdam Publishers, The Netherlands

info@amsterdampublishers.com

On Sunny Days We Sang is part of the series Holocaust Survivor True Stories WWII

Copyright © Jeannette Grunhaus de Gelman, 2022

Translated by Julia Shirek Smith from Spanish *En los días claros cantábamos*.

Cover image: Jenny Bemergui

CONTENTS

To the memory of my parents who – despite adversity – found the strength to rebuild their lives.

For my grandchildren, Gabriela, Alexandra and Jaime, Ariel and Daniela, Yael, Leah, and Meyer. May they take pride in belonging to a family and a people that survived to preserve their legacy.

Everything can be taken from a man but one thing: the last of the human freedoms – to choose one's attitude in any given set of circumstances, to choose one's own way.

Victor Frankl, Auschwitz Survivor (1946)

1

JUST US

From the time I was very young, a deep feeling of loneliness would often overwhelm me. I, Jeannette, the oldest of three, grew up in a small family in Maracaibo, Venezuela, with my parents and my brother and sister. Although my childhood was a happy one, I felt envious of my friends with large families – of their cousins, aunts, uncles, and above all their grandparents. This absence of extended family tormented me and the question of why it was just us was ever present in my mind. Eventually, I realized that the emptiness in our household had an explanation: most of my relatives, close and distant, had been murdered in Poland during the Second World War. My parents were the only survivors.

With this knowledge, a faint yet persistent gray shadow began to follow me, casting itself over me, materializing in an irrational hostility toward anything that had to do with Germany or Germans – they were to blame for my state of uneasiness. Oddly enough, such rejection did not extend to Poland or Poles, maybe because my mother used to recount with nostalgia anecdotes about her childhood and early youth, remembering happy moments from those stages of her existence. I have few recollections of tales and stories told by my father. My heart knew that my mother's sadness and my father's serious demeanor were the result of the traumatic experiences they had endured. The suffering, the pain, had a profound impact on their souls. Despite such deep wounds, they yearned for their vanished life and never completely adjusted to a new reality. I am sure that for them, more than for me, the loss of their family was a heavy burden to bear.

As I grew older the shadow began to fade away. I simply stopped paying attention to it. At home, the fear of hurting my parents by reawakening painful memories drove me from discussing the war in any depth. The subject was also not taken up with my brother or sister, or with anybody else. Yet seeing films or reading about the Holocaust made me cry. While strong emotions were then stirred in me, they were immediately pushed back, never confronted. For reasons I could not pinpoint or maybe did not want to know, I closed the door to my parents' past with a barrier I did not dare tamper with or tear down.

With the passing of time, the gray shadow grew even weaker and became barely noticeable. Once in a great while it would resurface, as it did during a short student trip when I passed through Warsaw, and on a second family trip the same summer when I consented to spend four days in Germany. While there, my reaction to the sights and sounds was intense. Hearing German spoken was terrifying, everyday expressions became sinister faces, music sounded like military marches, and the food revolted me. The tourist sites we visited did not interest me at all. The anguish that overtook me was so distressing I told myself I would never come back to Germany or Poland.

Many years later, and much to my surprise, my mother showed a desire to return to Poland on a trip organized by a group of survivors from Włodawa, her birthplace. Among those going would be her best friend and soul sister, Sara Omelinski. I also decided to go, along with my brother, Leo, and sister, Rosa. But before I even set foot on Polish soil the gray shadow reappeared, stronger than ever, and my anxiety hit a new high. Since my father's passing in 1997, my mother, my siblings and I, her eight grandchildren, and her great-granddaughter, had built a united and triumphant family. Telling myself we were no longer alone did not help. The fear that overcame me was out of control and would have to be tamed for me to face the trip. The thought of my mother reliving those dark times filled me with apprehension. I dreaded how she might react. But seeing her more than ready to undertake a journey to her past, that terrible past, I mustered up the courage to accompany her.

———

We took the trip in September of 2000. Each one of us coming from a different place. On the plane I gazed down at the landscape – green trees, green fields, small cities – but I could not focus on them. To my mind it was one big cemetery. Images of terror and death swirled in my head. We landed in Warsaw. At the airport, I examined the expression of every adult Pole, reading looks and gestures, speculating about what each of them might have done during the war. In the taxi, I forced myself to look out the window: manicured trees, buildings reminiscent of the communist past, modern structures, and brightly lit signs. My eyes were seeing a lively and restored city, but in my heart, Poland was and would always be gray, just gray.

I arrived at the hotel to find my sister Rosa already there. I hugged her, happy to see a familiar face at last. We ventured out to have dinner in the old city, completely rebuilt after the war. The evening was cool, with a slight breeze, and around us Poles and cheerful tourists were talking, laughing. I could see no trace of Jewish history anywhere in this area. Bewildered, I asked myself what was left of the 3.3 million Jews who were living in Poland in 1939. Despite being a part of the country's history, their legacy – their memory – seemed to have simply evaporated. I wondered if Poland was something else now … free, but without Jews.

I thought of my ancestors. It was as though they had never existed. But there I was, wanting confirmation of my family's origins, wanting to know the place where my parents came from, and to understand what their lives had been like. Never, until then, had these questions come to my mind. On that first night on Polish soil, I began to seek answers, not yet imagining that such a decision would awaken a pressing need to write the story of my parents and my entire family.

2

WŁODAWA THROUGH THE AGES

I always knew the town my family came from was called Włodawa. For me the name suggested nothing more than a point on the map, far away in eastern Poland on the Russian border, on a river, the Bug. Before our trip in 2000, I looked in the atlas and found Włodawa, there on the banks of the mysterious Bug, near the border where Poland meets the southwestern tip of Belarus and the northwestern tip of the Ukraine. It was in this *shtetl*[1] that my parents were born: Hil Grunhaus Beckerman (Chil Majer Gringauz Beckerman) and Alexandra Lederman Beckerman (Chana Szejndla Lederman Beckerman).[2]

The origins of Włodawa go back to the 13th century. From the 15th century on, it is referred to as a town owned by nobility. In the 16th century, it began to develop and became a center of commerce and crafts, obtaining municipal rights along with permission to set up weekly markets and four fairs each year. By 1531, there are already references to the presence of Jews in Włodawa, as Polish nobles were quite open to receiving them and allowed them to settle on their lands.

Due to various historical ups and downs the growth of the Jewish population was unsteady. The first documented pogrom occurred in

1684 when the Cossacks burned the town, massacring its inhabitants. Over time, however, Jews started returning. Between 1760 and 1780, Włodawa was revived due to privileges granted to all residents by the masters of the city, which also benefited the Jews. With the authorization to establish a Jewish quarter – which included a synagogue, a school, a butcher shop, a *mikvah* (ritual bath), and a complex of three buildings for religious purposes (which still stand today) – their community was soon thriving. At the same time, the institutions of communal government grew stronger under the *kehilla,* a governing body which lasted until the Second World War.

In 1795, a portion of Poland (including Włodawa), was annexed to the Austrian Empire, and in 1798 it fell under czarist domination. At the beginning of the 19th century, Włodawa underwent a period of economic stagnation until the building of a railroad gave a new impetus to development. Between the end of the 19th century and the early years of the 20th century, the city saw a certain degree of progress – especially in the center of town – with the arrival of electricity, the paving of some streets, plus the construction of substantial brick buildings.

Finally, in 1918, the year of the creation of the Second Polish Republic, Włodawa was no longer under Russian control and began to be ruled by Polish laws. Amidst all these changes, from 1820 on, Jews began to dominate the demographic structure of the city. The Jewish population gradually increased, keeping its position as the majority in relation to the number of Poles and other minorities. In 1939, Włodawa had 9,500 inhabitants of whom 5,600 (60 percent) were Jewish.

GRUNHAUS
FAMILY TREE

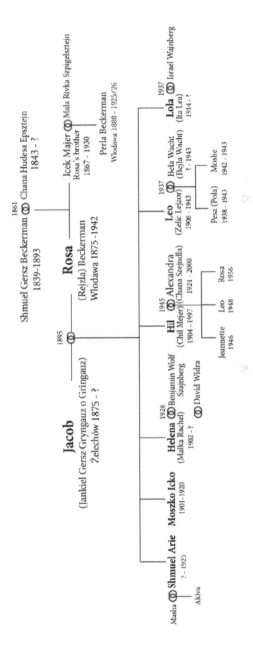

3

THE GRUNHAUS FAMILY

My paternal grandfather, Jacob Grunhaus (Jankiel Gersz Gryngauz or Gringauz), arrived in Włodawa in 1895 to marry Rosa (Rejzla) Beckerman. Jacob was born in 1875 in Żelechów, a small city located some 143 kilometers from Włodawa. Did he travel to Włodawa solely for a marriage arranged according to the old practice? Was he also seeking better economic opportunities? My father told us that his ancestors had arrived in Poland from Silesia in the middle of the 17th century and that they had been dedicated to working in lumber. That may be why my grandfather decided to settle in Włodawa where the biggest industry in the last years of the 19th century was processing wood, for local use and for export. The surname Grunhaus, Gryngauz, or Gringaus was not common in the city. It only seems to be linked to our family and to a sister of Grandfather Jacob named Feige, who also married and settled in Włodawa. Jacob had three brothers who ended up living in Warsaw.

My grandmother, Rosa Beckerman, was born in Włodawa in 1875. Her father, Shmuel Gersz Beckerman, born in 1839, was from Biała Podlaska, 76 kilometers northeast of Włodawa. Shmuel arrived there in 1861 to marry Chana Hudesa Epsztejn and make the city his home. Rosa had six siblings, who apparently resided there also. Beckerman or Bekierman was a fairly common surname in the region, and some Beckermans held important posts in the kehilla and in city government.

Jacob and Rosa had six children. The civil registry contains no record of the oldest, Shmuel Arie. There are only my father's memories of him, along with two photos, in which he looks very serious. Then came Moszko Icko in 1901; Helena (Malka Rachel) in 1902; my father, Hil (Chil Majer) in 1904; Leo (Zelic Lejzor), in 1906; and finally, Lola (Ita Leah) in 1914. They all grew up in the bosom of a well-off family, which was Orthodox, yet somewhat modern in its customs. In 1925, the firstborn, Shmuel Arie, barely 30, died of tuberculosis. He had married Masha, a cousin of the influential rabbi from Radzyń, and he left a son, Akiva, who went on living with his Grunhaus grandparents.

Jacob was a man of medium height, with blond hair, a mustache, a neatly trimmed beard, and a cheerful expression. Most of the children inherited his coloring. Rosa, on the other hand, looked severe with her short, dark wig. Strictly observant, she saw to it that the children recited their morning prayers before leaving for school. On Fridays and religious holidays, she would light the candles and prepare the house for the *Shabbat*. Rosa held a permanent position in the synagogue as the *gabete,* with the responsibility of maintaining order in the section where the women prayed. And since she was strongly pious, people called upon her to present their prayers in the cemetery or ask for aid to the sick.

The Grunhaus family home at 46 Wyrykowska Street, was a large and comfortable one-story frame house with eight rooms. In addition, there was a warehouse, a storage shed, and a 600-square-foot garden. In 1932, the family already had a telephone, listed as number 54.

Grandfather Jacob

Grandmother Rosa

Shmuel

Akiva

Until 1918 Włodawa was part of the Settlement Zone of the Russian Empire, and under Russian control Jews were limited socially and economically. With the founding of the Second Polish Republic new institutions were created, opening a brighter future for all. Jacob was an enterprising man who could envisage the possibilities emerging in the new Poland. Beginning in 1919 several references to his commercial activities appear in Polish records, all of them having to do with wood. In 1921, he began a six-year rental of some pieces of land in Tomaszówka, on the other side of the Bug River, in what is now Belarus. Between 1928 and 1930 he gradually bought up these plots, on which he established a large sawmill. In a 1928 yearbook he is listed as a lumber merchant; in the 1930 Włodawa-Domaczewo industrial directory as a timber industrialist; and in the 1931–1932 Włodawa telephone book as a "dealer in forestry products." In that publication, the surname appears as Grünhaus, as my father would go on writing it, minus the umlaut.

Clearly the Jewish majority had an influence on life in Włodawa. For the most part, the Jewish residents dwelled in the downtown area around the *rynek* (market square). Shops and grocery stores could be found in that part of town, grouped according to the type of merchandise offered. The non-Jewish population tended to reside in the outlying areas. In general, the Jews were shopkeepers or artisans and some – not many – owned farms. Jewish business owners were a minority in the town, even if 85 percent of the small industries (the mills, the electric company, the print shops) were the property of Jews. As in all shtetls, sources of employment were limited and most of the Jewish population existed in great poverty.

In the early years of the 20th century, Włodawa and the surrounding areas had a dozen *Hasidic* (ultra-Orthodox) groups, each gravitating around the figure of a rabbi as their spiritual and intellectual leader. Eighty percent of the population was Orthodox, as in most of the shtetls and small cities of eastern Poland, with religion marking the communities' way of life. Politically speaking, in Włodawa (and the rest of Poland) the Agudat Israel Party organized and represented the *Hasidim.* Its main objective was the protection of the rights and religious freedoms of the Orthodox community. Along with this, toward the end of the 19th-century Zionist ideas had begun to reach Włodawa. By 1920, three political groups officially represented Zionism and 1922 saw the founding of the largest Zionist youth movement, known as Hashomer Hatzair. Since the movement's main focus was to encourage emigration to Palestine, many of its activities centered on preparing local young people for a future there. In the 1930s the Włodawa area branch had three working farms with about 300 recruits. When youth from other regions began arriving, it was necessary to go across the Bug River to Tomaszówka to set up a *kibbutz* (collective farm). There, the young participants worked the land and went off to town to sell their produce. They distinguished themselves by wearing khaki uniforms.

Jacob identified with the Zionist ideals, clearly understanding the movement's philosophies, and managed to integrate them into his Orthodox beliefs. We know this because my father talked about it but also because Jacob is mentioned in the survivor's accounts which describe him as religious yet modern and a Zionist. Jacob was greatly respected in Włodawa and an influential participant in the city's economic and political institutions. Beginning in 1918, with the establishment of the Polish Republic, Jews had legal status as citizens, meaning they could exercise their vote in three elections: for the Polish parliament, for local city offices, and for their kehilla. Thus, in 1918 the first officially established community council was elected: an eight-member group with Jacob Grunhaus as chairman. The city authorities did not exactly endorse this council due to its markedly Zionist slant, but it went on functioning de facto until the next election, which was held in 1924. The local authorities distrusted the Zionists who were trying to awaken a social conscience as well as a nationalism directed toward Palestine.

As chairman of the kehilla, in 1920 Jacob found himself facing a harsh test. The troops of General Stanisław Bulak-Balachowicz, supposedly battling the Communists who had overthrown the czar of Russia, moved into the Włodawa area. They organized break-ins and pogroms aimed at Jews. Committing these violent acts, they murdered 126 Jews in the city and in the surrounding localities. Among their victims was Moszko Icko, Grandfather Jacob's son, just 19 years old. The army also ordered Jacob, as head of the community, to round up 10 cubic meters of hay for their cavalry within three hours or they would hang ten Jews. Fortunately, the soldiers had to abandon Włodawa quite suddenly, and they were unable to carry out this threat.

Włodawa exemplified the changes occurring in the shtetls of the new Poland. The city's Polish and Jewish communities coexisted without much contact. In a census conducted in 1931, between 70 and 85 percent of Jews marked either Yiddish or Hebrew as their mother tongue; regardless, many Jews, especially those taking up the new political trends, participated in civic institutions. Włodawa had a Jewish mayor from 1915 to 1916 and in 1925 eight Jews were elected to the 18-member city council. Jews, however, were not allowed to participate in the district government. As an exception, in 1927 Jacob Grunhaus became one of the city's two representatives on the district council. Christians in Włodawa – despite being the minority percentage wise – still ran the city including the government, the police force, and the civil service.

My parents used to mention with pride the strong social conscience of Włodawa's kehilla which supported charitable, cultural, and educational activities. It maintained two synagogues, several *shtiebelej* (prayer houses), a mikvah, and three cemeteries. It subsidized numerous *hederim* (religious primary schools), a *Talmud Torah* (religious school for the upper grades), and an orphanage. It also collected taxes from those who could pay, using the money to aid the neediest inhabitants in all aspects – providing them with food, clothing, and health care. The kehilla also maintained the Chevra Kadisha, a burial society; provided care for the sick through the Bikur Cholim; helped young women prepare for marriage and set up a household with the Hachnosas Kallah; and offered help and hospitality to indigents and travelers via the Hachnosas Orchim. For all these tasks the kehilla received aid from the city government. In addition, the Kupat Gmiluth Hessed – a cooperative bank accountable to the kehilla – oversaw commercial activities in the Włodawa Jewish community.

Grandfather Jacob was an open, compassionate, and generous person. He loved and took great care of his family, while at the same time showing great sympathy for the needy. All this could be seen in his active concern for the members of the kehilla, which he demonstrated through his political participation and his aid and support for various projects and charitable institutions. From 1916 on he was a member of a committee that aided the refugees who had begun coming to the city. Most notably, this group received, fed, gave lodging to, and cared for the children who arrived in the period between the two wars.

Jacob's Zionist ideals were made evident in 1924 when he allowed his son Hil to emigrate to Palestine using one of three legal visas given in Włodawa. Later, in 1930, with a group of wood merchants, he helped erect a building on Przechodnia Street which served as the headquarters of the Zionist organizations. This structure became the center of community activities for all the Jewish institutions in the city. With the same spirit of generosity, a few years earlier he had spearheaded the building of a small *Beit Hamidrash* (study center) for a Hasidic group.

Jacob and Rosa were very observant. It's possible that their children gradually distanced themselves from such rigid Orthodoxy. In many photos we see Helena and Lola without wigs: two beautiful blondes with long, wavy hair, dressed elegantly in stylish short-sleeved gowns that leave their arms bare, defying the strict religious dress code. Then there are the pictures of Hil and Leo, with neither wearing any head covering. Leo closely resembles his brother but younger and taller. They are both blonde, their expressions open and natural. The siblings appear in photos taken in the house, at the sawmill, strolling through town, and with family. They all have happy smiles – no one has a premonition of what the future will bring.

Hil, my father, had great admiration and respect for his father, Jacob, and was strongly influenced by his thinking and character. There was a story my father liked to tell. Włodawa had a movie theatre, yet Jacob had never seen a film. Sometime between 1928 and 1939 when Hil was living in Gdynia, Jacob came for a visit and the two of them went to the movies. They saw a Charlie Chaplin film, which both thoroughly enjoyed.

Lola, Helena and Hil

Leo and Hil

Akiva, Lola, Helena

Bela, Lola, Leo, Israel

Helena and David Widra

Lola and Israel

By 1939, the year the war broke out, three of my father's siblings were already married. In 1936, Helena (Malka) wed Benjamin Wolf Szajnberg, and it seems that later she married David Widra (Vidra). In 1937, Leo married Bajla (Bela) Wacht, and the same year Lola became the bride of Israel Wajnberg. Helena's marital history is somewhat unclear. Although a certificate of her marriage to Benjamin Wolf has turned up, my father never told us about this union. Every time he talked about Helena, he referred to her as the wife of David Widra. And indeed, there are several photos of the two, either as a couple or in a family group. It is also a fact that David Widra worked with my father in Gdynia. Perhaps Helena was widowed and then made this second marriage, but no record of Benjamin's death has been found. Helena and David moved to Białystok, Lola and Israel settled in Kovel, and Leo and Bela in Włodawa. In 1938, Leo and Bela had a daughter, Pola (Pesa), and in 1942 they had a son, Moses. Neither of my father's two sisters had children by 1939.

LEDERMAN
FAMILY TREE

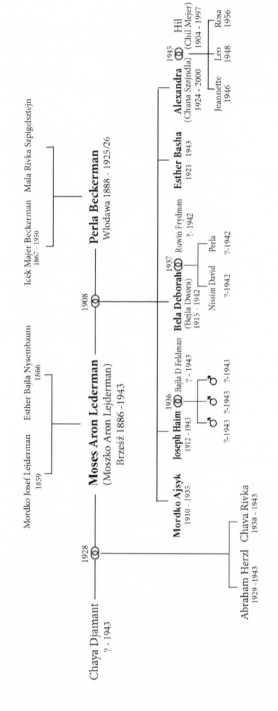

4

THE LEDERMAN FAMILY

While we discovered many references to Jacob Grunhaus's role as a community leader, we did not find out much about my mother's family. That may be because my maternal grandfather, Moses Aron, being Hasidic and leading a life centered around religion, participated less in the political and social doings in Włodawa. And adding to that, my maternal grandmother, Perla Beckerman, died when my mother was a little girl.

Moses Aron Lederman (Moszko Aron Lejderman) was born in 1886 in Brześć (now Brest) in Belarus, 73 kilometers north of Włodawa. It is uncertain when he arrived in Włodawa, but we believe his family settled there in the middle of the 19th century. He had several siblings in the city. My mother mentioned at least two Lederman first cousins on her father's side: Yankel and Haskel Lederman, both sons of Gerzon Enoch. The surname Lederman was quite common in the area.

In 1904, Moses Aron married his first wife, Cyrla Sztilerman who died a few years later, leaving him a childless widower. In 1908, he wed my grandmother, Perla Beckerman who was born in Włodawa in 1888. Perla's father, Icek Majer Beckerman, was born in 1867. He was the brother of my paternal grandmother, Rosa Beckerman. Icek's wife was Mala Rivka Szpigelsztein from Białystok. Moses and Perla had five children. Mordko Ajsyk was born in 1910, Joseph Haim in 1912, Bajla Deborah in 1915, Esther Basha in 1921, and Alexandra (Chana Szejndla) – my mother – in 1924. My parents were second cousins.

The Ledermans, like the Beckermans, were well known in Włodawa. Perla came from a well-off, middle-class family; her parents had a small building in the rynek with five shops. One of them, number 22, Moses had bought from Abraham Bekierman in 1924. In the front was the store which was adjacent to the property of my mother's grandfather, Icek Majer, and in the rear were two apartments without attics. My mother and her family did not live there but in a house on Błotna Street. Perla died in 1925 or 1926. My mother did not know the exact date of her death or the cause. Moses, now a widower with small children, soon married for a third time. He and his wife, Chaya Djamant, had two children. Abraham Herzl was born in 1929, Chava Rivka in 1938.

My mother spoke affectionately of her father, Moses Aron, whom she remembered as being observant. He was a faithful follower of the Radzyń rabbi. When there was an important religious holiday, such as the Jewish New Year, Moses would go to Radzyń Podlaski, the rabbi's city, some 82 kilometers from Włodawa. For other holidays when no one worked, Włodawa had a house where Moses could join other Radzyń Hasidim to pray and study the sacred books. His daily routine revolved around the three traditional daily prayer times: morning, afternoon, and night. He would rise at four, study until six, go to the synagogue, then head to his place of work. Moses is listed in the 1928 telephone directory as a grocery store owner. My mother described him as a quiet man, devoted to his religion and concerned about his family: "My father was not a big talker. He was constantly studying, yet he noticed everything happening in the house, and if you did something inappropriate, you would hear about it." His rabbi was a spiritual guide as well as an adviser on practical matters. When Moses faced a problem, he would consult the rabbi about the path to follow. He valued this advice so much that it often helped him overcome difficulties. My mother told about her little brother

Abraham Herzl being ill with lung problems each winter. One year, after he had spent several weeks in bed with a fever and no improvement, Moses turned to the rabbi, who advised him to take the child to Lublin, a bigger city, and consult a doctor about the feasibility of performing surgery. And it was done. They removed two of the child's ribs, which saved him. The rabbi's advice had been good indeed.

Despite being thoroughly traditional and conservative, Moses Aron understood the importance of a comprehensive education. And what is surprising for his time and social milieu, is that this included the education of women. Following the guidelines of the Radzyń rabbi, who supported the creation of *Beit Yaakov* schools for girls and young women, Moses was one of the founders of Włodawa's Beit Yaakov. The purpose of such schools was to give women a more complete education within the parameters of Orthodoxy, and to counteract the assimilating influence of the Polish environment. Young girls and adolescents who went to a Polish public school would go to Beit Yaakov in the afternoon to round out their education. Here they would study reading and writing, Jewish history and holy texts, all in Yiddish.

Boys between the ages of 5 and 12 would attend a *heder* to study with a rabbi or a teacher, known in a heder as the *melamed*. These schools usually operated in the melamed's home, and the instruction was in Yiddish. There are many tales – some famous and some not – about these *melamdim,* that tell of how they treated their students, how they punished them, and so on. One thing beyond doubt is that they were a major element in the education of young boys in the shtetls. The year 1922 saw the founding of the Beit Yosef secondary school where young men could pursue their heder studies up to the age of 18. Originally there had been other schools as well, such as the Talmud Torah, which was subsidized by the kehilla. These were places where boys, especially those with limited resources, could receive a religious education. The brightest students would enter a *yeshiva* at the age of 12 or 13 and remain there until they were 19, studying the most advanced holy texts. In general, formal education would end when young men had to look for work.

Many Jewish children attended Polish public schools; however, most observant parents tried to avoid sending their male children to these institutions because there they were not allowed to cover their heads as required by Jewish tradition. Nonetheless, the number of Jews receiving a public education gradually increased. By the 1937–1938 school year Jewish children made up 52 percent of the student population. Few went on to higher education. Instead, they were likely to enroll in a community vocational school to learn various trades: tailoring, shoemaking, carpentry, etc. The first post-secondary school in Włodawa opened in 1937.

With the introduction of Zionist ideas in the city, some Jews demanded the modification of the educational system to allow for schooling less tied to Orthodox Judaism. Beginning in 1914, under the sponsorship of the Zionists, Hebrew classes were taught at a Tarbut Movement institution, which became an official school in 1922, with five grades (and later seven) that corresponded to those of an elementary school. The Włodawa Tarbut offered night classes for adults, with some 90 students in attendance by the time the war started.

The religious and political diversity present in Włodawa, like that in many other Polish shtetls, was a source of conflict for Moses Aron. He had to confront modern and reformist ideas in his own household. My uncle, Mordko Ajsyk, who did not want to be religious, argued with his father constantly, and became the leader of one of the Zionist movements – the Betar Organization.[1] Mordko upset his father by leaving home for an encampment on the outskirts of Włodawa that was occupied by young people preparing themselves to leave for Palestine. All were self-supporting and did heavy work even in the middle of winter. They ate poorly, which may be why my uncle contracted tuberculosis. His father, concerned, sent him to a sanatorium but Mordko could not be cured and died in 1935, barely 24 years old. His brother Joseph, on the other hand, pursued religious studies diligently. He traveled to Warsaw to attend a yeshiva since one was not available in Włodawa, completed the training required to become a rabbi, then decided not to practice.

By 1939, at the start of the war, Joseph and his wife, Bajla Dewora Feldman, whom he had married in 1936, were the parents of three children. Deborah had married Ruwin Frydman in 1937, and the couple had a daughter, Perla. Esther was single, as was my mother, both living with their father and his third wife, Chaya, and the couple's two young children.

I try to visualize my mother's family but without photographs it is hard. Perla's face floats in the air, vague. Moses Aron and Joseph are wearing Hasidic garb: round fur hats, white shirts with collars, long black jackets with trousers, *tzitzit* (knotted fringes) dangling from their waists, long untidy beards, *payot* (corkscrew curls) hanging from their temples. I see Mordko Ajsyk in shirt and trousers with no beard or payot. The women go along modestly with long sleeves and high collars. My mother is quite pretty. She has dark hair pulled back, a fair complexion and a playful expression. Esther's hair is close to blonde. She is smiling, but I cannot picture Deborah or Esther's faces.

5

THE BUG RIVER, SILENT WITNESS

My mother, Alexandra (or Scheindele, as they called her in Włodawa) was born on December 21, 1924,[1] on the first night of *Hanukkah,* the Festival of Lights. She was the youngest of five children. Not long after she was born her mother, Perla, passed away. My mother sometimes said she had died of an infection because there were no proper medications available, and she also mentioned tuberculosis. In the 1930 civil registry Moses certifies that Perla died in Lublin on October 19, 1925. This leads me to believe that she may have fallen ill after the delivery and was treated in Lublin where there were better doctors and hospitals.

Alexandra grew up with the sense of being an orphan. She would often mention her siblings, yet never go into detail about how they got along with one other. And she never described her relationship with her stepmother, who for all practical purposes raised her. I do not recall her saying much about Chaya, other than that she was her father's wife. Sometimes she spoke of her sister, Deborah, who at times ran the household, and more often of her sister Esther, who was her companion. And it is true that she was quite fond of her maternal grandmother, Mala Rivka. They saw each other once a week, going out together to walk across the bridge to Tomaszówka and Włodawka, two shtetls on the other side of the Bug River. Mala Rivka must have been a warm and loving grandmother. She died before the war, and her husband Icek Majer Beckerman passed away in 1930. Both had come from large families, with Icek himself one of six children, meaning that my mother ended up with many cousins. She never knew her paternal grandparents.

Włodawa was the largest shtetl in the area. From early in the century, most buildings around the market square (or rynek) were of brick, some of them two stories with balconies, although there were still quite a number of frame houses. A few streets were paved by this time. In the downtown area stood another building, rectangular, with two exits and a patio in the middle. People called this structure the Czworobok or Brom. It contained 37 shops, side by side, mostly Jewish owned, like almost all the stores on the rynek.

Moses Aron would often go to Chelm and Lublin to buy food products and other merchandise for his shop, which was in a small building with the five stores belonging to the Beckerman family. My mother never explained why the Ledermans, unlike some of the Beckermans, did not reside behind their place of business. Rather, they lived on Błotna Street alongside other family members in a house they did not own, "where we were all family."

Thursday was the liveliest day of the week since there would regularly be a market in the rynek (unless it happened to be a Jewish holiday). A multitude of farmers from the surrounding area would invade the square – their wagons bringing wheat, cheese, chickens and eggs, and meat and fish. And in turn they would scour the Jewish shops, hunting for whatever they might need: fabric, shoes, skins, leather goods, farm implements. The hustle and bustle were grand, with much movement to and fro. And since most of the people depended on these exchanges for their livelihood, they would take advantage of market day to establish or reinforce mutual contacts.

The rynex on market day (Wlodawa Museum)

As a little girl, my mother loved to play. We would often listen to her happy recollections of childhood pastimes: "Our winters were fierce, and sometimes it would go down to more than 20 degrees below zero, but we kids ignored the cold. We would go out, play with the snow, build snowmen. There was a little hill and since I had a sled, I would slide down it even when the temperature was very low." Once back inside the house, when nighttime came, she always wanted her bed to be warmed before she went to sleep, which was just a part of life in that frigid climate. In the summertime she would play outside on the communal patio with friends and family.

For *Rosh Hashanah* and *Passover*, it was customary to buy new clothes for the older children. Since families were generally large and did not have a lot of money, they bought none for the younger children, who would be getting their siblings' hand-me-downs. That is what happened to little Alexandra time after time since she was the youngest daughter. Those who did not have something new to wear for a holiday would usually get a fresh piece of fruit of the season. This tradition was quite deeply rooted, and in fact, Grandmother Mala Rivka told Alexandra that when she was old enough, they took her to see the rabbi, who told her, "Now you can start wearing new outfits." To underline the great importance of this meeting, he gave her a lump of sugar, which she sucked on all the way home, quite excited. This tradition was engraved in my mother's memory, and she observed it during my childhood in Maracaibo. I would be thrilled when a Jewish holiday came, and I had something new to put on.

The boys in the family attended the heder from the age of three. Education was mandatory in Poland, and the government recognized that type of schooling. Girls had to go to the public school. Alexandra's school was on Piłsudskiego Street. In the afternoons she studied at the local Beit Yaakov, founded by her father. A studious, sensible little girl, she enjoyed both schools, recalling in later years having been an excellent student who received good grades. "I never had problems with my schoolwork," she often stated. In the registries for the public school, her name appears from the first to the fifth grade.

Half the students in her class were Jewish, and on the Shabbat they did not attend. Alexandra had a non-Jewish friend and the two would get together on Sundays to go over the missed lessons. She talked about this girl fondly and considered her a good friend. Despite the number of Poles at the school, there was little contact between Jewish and Polish children. As my mother explained, "Half the class was Polish, the other half, Jewish. There were about 50 students, which meant you would have enough friends among the Jews."

It seems that her sister Esther was not quite the scholar that Alexandra was. Since Esther was older, at one point she offered to do some of her little sister's homework. My mother recounted the incident, amused: "Esther did a bad job of it, and I got a low grade, which had never happened before. I was mad, and I never let her do my homework again."

From early childhood my mother was an avid reader, frequently visiting the public library to check out books. She started with simple works, like *Heart* by Edmondo de Amicis, which was her first favorite, later becoming devoted to many Polish authors, among them Henryk Seinkiewicz. During the war, when she was confined to an apartment in Warsaw for nearly a year, she did nothing but read. A love of literature continued throughout her existence. Our house was full of books, as both my parents read a lot. We children, and later the grandchildren, all inherited this interest. Influenced by my mother, *Through the Desert* (one of Sienkiewicz's works) and *Heart* were among my first books.

My mother felt much love and admiration for her father. She respected him greatly and valued his integrity and his dedication to religion and study: "My father had many Hasidic friends. During the week, at the shtiebelej they would recite the three daily prayers together. On the day they did not work they would get together to study the *Torah* and discuss the commentaries on the Talmud." That Moses had been instrumental in establishing a Beit Yaakov school for girls in Włodawa filled her with pride. She declared emphatically that the school was "outstanding and taught many subjects – reading and writing, Jewish history, grammar, literature, secular subjects, all sorts of things – with religion as the base. It was organized by levels, and when you finished them all, you would graduate. Lessons were in Yiddish, and in Hebrew too. The teachers were excellent. They had been brought from Vilna."

Alexandra spoke well Yiddish and Polish since she studied in both languages. Having finished her seven years of elementary school, her father enrolled her in private classes to study "things like typing" but the war broke out and she could not continue. Moses Aron's support of education for women was way ahead of his time. It is also remarkable that he let a daughter read nonreligious books by Polish authors.

During the week, once she had done her homework, young Alexandra would play in the neighborhood. Coming from such a big family, she had many aunts and uncles and cousins living close by. There were frequent visits back and forth, and the children grew up together. On Saturdays the whole town went out walking, some going as far as the Bug River. The town's principal thoroughfare, Piłsudskiego Street, with its chestnut trees and inviting benches, was a lovely central meeting place on weekends. In the city park the children ran about among the leafy trees while the adults chatted. On the outskirts of town there were wooded areas where Alexandra and her friends would pick raspberries, blackberries, and mushrooms in the spring and summer. "It was so pretty. There were woods, there were farmers' fields, you could take a peaceful walk down to the river. We were all so happy to be out in the open air ... I would have such a good time." Those recollections of her childhood and youth were a recurrent subject, and it delighted her to relive them.

On Friday night and Saturday, the girls went to Beit Yaakov to say the Shabbat prayers. Alexandra knew them by heart and understood their meaning perfectly. Throughout the year, Beit Yaakov had a bit of control over the way the community celebrated religious holidays. For Hanukkah and *Purim*, the students would put together elaborate entertainments. They would rent the movie theatre and sell tickets. The performances were nice because the most talented girls were chosen to sing, recite, and dance. When Purim came, the young people would dress in costumes and go from door to door seeking money for charitable causes.

As in any shtetl, the Jewish-owned stores in Włodawa closed for Shabbat and the Jewish holidays. "There were some who were not religious, but the majority were. Everybody had to close. They would go down the streets on Friday, saying 'Close the stores, close the stores.'" And then people went to pray in the synagogue or the shtiebelej. On Saturdays the activity in the shtetl came to a halt.

Young Alexandra was closer to her sister Esther than to Deborah, who was much older. Esther loved to eat, becoming rather plump. Lively and intelligent, she was also determined, daring, and fearless. When their father required a helper at the store, he would invariably choose Esther. Her little sister adored her and admired that enterprising spirit. It was probably when the two of them reached adolescence that Alexandra, in need of a mother figure, began to listen to Esther. After their mother died, it was Deborah, then just II, who had to take on the heavier household chores. My mother spoke fondly of her efforts to make bread, struggling to reach the counter to knead the dough. That must have happened before their father remarried. Many years later, as I was growing up, I was often told how much my personality resembled Esther's.

Alexandra was also quite attached to her little brother, Abraham Herzl, who was five years her junior. The two spent much time together. In the summer, their father would rent a room in the house of a religious family in Włodawka, a shtetl located across the Bug River, so she and Abrumale (Abraham's nickname) could have a little vacation. She recalled them sharing pleasant days there. They went for walks, amused themselves, bought food. On Sundays, their father would visit to see how they were doing and bring them provisions. She enjoyed those stays so much!

My mother did not reminisce much about her other siblings. She admired Mordko Ajsyk who had the courage to pursue his ideal and was trying to leave Włodawa. Unfortunately, when he was all set to go, Palestine put a halt to immigration, and while waiting for another opportunity, he fell ill and died. She never did talk about Joseph, as he was much older and rarely home (he spent several years away studying in Warsaw). Memories of Deborah were more vivid, perhaps because they were both women. She had little to say about her siblings' weddings but did recall her father going to Lublin to sell his late wife's jewelry so that he could buy two watches as wedding gifts: one for Deborah, the other for Joseph's bride.

Włodawa's harsh winters called for some sizeable expenditures. With the big families many had back in those days, clothing was a significant expense. On top of this, living quarters had to be heated. "You could not exist without heating. Houses were small, in the center you had a wood-burning stove that served all the rooms. You put wood in it, and when you were through, you closed the heavy little door and that way the whole house would get heated." Sometimes a fire had to be lit both morning and night. On Friday night and Saturday, when Orthodox Jews do not light fires, a Polish woman would come and walk from house to house starting up the stoves. After doing the whole street, she returned to each dwelling

32

and shut the stove door. She knew exactly what to do since on the Shabbat giving instructions was not allowed.

My mother repeated time and time again that Włodawa, being a small city, did not have many job opportunities. There were about 20 rich families, with the rest of the people middle class or poor. "If you had a roof over your heads, if you had money for food and clothing, you were middle class. Otherwise, you were poor." That is why the institutions of community aid were so important – they supplied many necessities.

One of her most poignant memories was of the great solidarity among the community's members: "The community was well organized. People would help one another." On Fridays, the girls went from house to house collecting bread and money for the poor. When programs were put on at school, proceeds from the ticket sales went to charity. The community took care of orphans, the ailing, and the needy through various institutions. It provided aid to young women from humble families when they became engaged, enabling them to marry. All this within a framework of widespread poverty: "To subsist was quite difficult for most people." The will to help others stayed with my mother throughout her life. She found it important to work for Jewish and non-Jewish institutions that helped those in need.

If you asked my mother about antisemitism, she would reply that it most definitely existed. To her, the Poles were born with such sentiments: "Perhaps at home they heard contemptuous talk about Jews. I do not understand why antisemitism was so deep-rooted. You perceived it every day. However, we had to survive, and that was not easy, so we did not focus on it." Nevertheless, she did not recall any antisemitic incidents in Włodawa. At the public schools, sometimes the kids would call one of them *żydówka*, that is, "Jewish girl." Once, when students complained to the teacher, the answer was that the Polish children were not saying anything bad, they were simply stating the fact that they were Jews. Still, Alexandra suspected they were doing so with contempt. But other than those occasions, she did not recall having been rejected by Poles, partly because her contact with non-Jews was limited.

In the prewar years, mostly starting in 1935, virulent antisemitism reemerged all over Poland. Alexandra never faced antisemitic acts directly. She remembered hearing the propaganda of the *Endeks* (members of the National Democratic Party) who called for the boycotting of Jewish stores and incited acts of physical violence against Jews. No such terrifying episodes occurred in Włodawa, although incidents were reported in places nearby. For example, 50 kilometers away in Parczew there were several attempts of forced conversion, and in 1932 a violent anti-Jewish uprising took place.

My mother was nearly 15 when the war broke out and her world was abruptly destroyed. Her life up to that point remained sealed in her memory. In her later years, she talked to us longingly of her routines and her experiences, her family and her community: the innocent and happy years of her childhood.

Bug River, June 2017 (Photo by the author)

6

A COSMOPOLITAN JEW

Hil Grunhaus Beckerman, my father, was born in Włodawa on January 3, 1904, and grew up in a city that would be under Russian domination until 1918. He shared few details of his childhood and youth. As a father he was so serious that I had to try hard to picture him as a child, playing or going to school. He most certainly attended the heder as all the Jewish boys did in Włodawa. During those early years, Russian school inspectors would check to see that the children in the hederim had a smattering of Russian, which means he probably learned a little of that language. Unquestionably, he had been well educated. We wonder if that might have been partly due to his attending the classes of Eli Schreiber Rosenblum – a Zionist melamed who taught writing, calligraphy, reading, and mathematics, all in Yiddish. And indeed, my father's Yiddish penmanship was impeccable. In Spanish, too, his cursive script was concise and elegant – like his Yiddish writing. Also, he spoke Hebrew and Polish fluently and knew some German. At home, Yiddish was spoken and apparently German too. How or where he acquired Polish fluency is not recorded, since he explained once that the Polish public education system was not created until 1918, and only included primary grades until 1928, a little late for him to have benefitted from them. Nonetheless, his command of Polish was excellent, without it he would not have survived the war.

In his own words, my father described the typical day from his boyhood: "Get up, wash, morning prayers, breakfast, and off to the heder. All this under the watchful eye of my mother."[1] After school it was homework, playing in the park with friends (if there was time), or he might help with household chores. The Shabbat was celebrated according to the practices of Orthodox families. Rosa would light the candles and the boys would go to the synagogue with their father. Once back home, they would have a family dinner. Saturday was similar: all Orthodox Jews went to the synagogue in the morning, the afternoon and later without fail had the customary festive meal or *seder (seudah)*.

In 1920, when my father was just 16, a tragedy struck his family. His brother, Moszko Icko, who was working at the sawmill in Towaszówka, fell victim to the violence of the troops of General Bulak-Balachowicz. These forces had arrived in the Włodawa area, where they (joined by Polish groups) fought the communists and killed anyone who crossed their path. My father remembered with great sadness the grief lived during those days in the Grunhaus household with the murder of his brother. As for the community, the fear and the hardships caused by the Balachowicz invasion slowly faded away.

As my father came to adopt the Zionist ideals spreading in Włodawa, he began to distance himself from Orthodox practices, dedicating himself fully to activities sponsored by Zionist groups. He was a nice-looking young man, blond and elegant. He was an activist, following his father's example with commitment to the kehilla and civic participation. Beginning in 1921 (at the age of 17), he served the first of two terms as secretary of the Zionist Organization and was also the representative of its Keren Kayemet LeIsrael group – which collected money for planting trees in Palestine. In Włodawa's *Yizkor Book*[2] there are several photos of my father with different groups of young people, all members of Zionist organizations. The commentary appearing with one of the pictures of the "Activists of the Keren Kayemet LeIsrael" is significant:[3] For these young people the Zionist movement was of the utmost importance, on a par with the Shabbat and religious holidays. In another photo, some boys are holding Keren Kayemet coin banks, which shows that back then these were already in use to collect money for Israel, just as we did years later in our house in Maracaibo.

Activists of the Keren Kayemet LeIsrael (Yiskor Book)

By the early 1920s, Włodawa already had cultural and social movements, mainly sponsored by various political parties. The year 1922 saw the founding of the Maccabi Sports Club. With its energetic soccer team, the Maccabi challenged other Jewish clubs in Brest, Chelm, and Lublin, as well as Włodawa's Polish teams. Many of the city's young people supported them. In 1926, an orchestra with 45 musicians was formed, giving regular concerts. Włodawa also had an active theatre group, a large library, and famous lecturers often came to town. In his article in the *Yizkor Book*, my father mentions all these groups and events and shows his pride in the cultural and political activities of "his city."

Comparing the early years of my father with those of my mother serves to highlight the difference between the two lifestyles present in Poland's Jewish world. In a rigid society just opening to modernity, two opposite extremes coexisted. My mother's youth revolved around religion, while my father's younger years revolved around Zionist ideas.

In 1924, Hil's leanings led to his being granted one of only three legal visas to travel to Palestine that were allotted to residents of Włodawa. Although many people had managed to emigrate illegally before then, this was the first time anyone in the city had been granted official authorization to make *Aliyah* – the journey to Palestine. Hil's decision to leave his family and city did not come about from the desire to seek a better economic situation, for he was from a well-off background. Certainly, he made his choice out of idealism and his strong Zionist convictions.

In other parts of Poland, many were being granted visas. In Włodawa, the news gave rise to jubilation, and the three recipients got ready to travel in December of 1924. On the eve of their departure the whole city came together for a farewell party complete with speeches, music, and dancing. Zishe Fuchs, one of those leaving, described the enthusiasm shown by the Zionist activists: "Blue and white flags adorned the walls of the hall. The atmosphere was one of joy and excitement. A lot of people were there. The singing and dancing lasted until dawn. Speeches, too. We were embarking on a mission that would give our lives meaning: populating the land of Israel."[4] The next morning the partygoers, still singing in Hebrew and Yiddish, escorted the three of them to the railroad station.

When the travelers arrived in Warsaw, they joined up with more emigrants who were heading for the train. They were surrounded by hundreds of enthusiasts who were there to bid them farewell. A festive atmosphere reigned at the station. Once again there were songs and dances and overwhelming excitement. Nonetheless, Zishe Fuchs could see the cynical glances of Polish onlookers who appeared to be thinking, *leave Jews, leave* – a clear expression of the antisemitism then prevalent in Poland. Finally, the travelers left, heading for Constanța, Romania. There they boarded a ship en route to the port of Jaffa, in Palestine, where they would be welcomed by earlier immigrants from Włodawa who would help them get settled.

We do not know the details of my father's years in Israel. He resided in Tel Aviv, probably near Rothschild Street (a main thoroughfare) which we suspect because whenever our family visited Israel, he would ask to take a walk in that part of town. He used to tell my siblings, Rosa and Leo, that it pleased him to have stayed in the first Jewish city. My parents' friendship with Zishe Fuchs lasted all their lives. We spent time with him on our trips to Israel: a tall white-haired man who was pleasant and always smiling.

In 1926, Hil returned to Włodawa. Once he mentioned to us that he came home to fulfill his military obligation but perhaps it was also to help his father with the sawmill after his brother, Shmuel Arie, died of tuberculosis in 1925. In the end, Hil got an exemption from military duty although it appears that he slept in the barracks for a short time. He remembered, laughing, that while he was there, 10 kilometers from Włodawa, his dog came looking for him one night, awakening his surprised master with a lick on the ear. My father was fond of dogs, and for a while we had one in Maracaibo that terrified me.

In 1928, Hil moved to Danzig (now Gdańsk), opening a sawmill in Gdynia. These two northern cities, just 25 kilometers apart on the Baltic, were ports strategically located for exporting goods. At that time, Danzig was a free city under the protection of the League of Nations from 1920 to 1929, and Poland, to counteract its influence, developed the port at Gdynia.

Logging was widespread in the Włodawa area. Many of the surrounding towns on the Bug used the long sandy stretches along the riverbank to store lumber over the winter. When the spring thaw came, workers tied the wood to special rafts they sent down the Bug to the Vistula River, and from there it went on to Danzig for export.

Hil, who was shrewd and saw the possibilities for growth, created a complex of operations devoted to wood. His father would send wood from Tomaszówka, which Hil would receive and process in Gdynia where he had a sawmill, workshops, and a warehouse. Every day Hil went back and forth between Gdynia and his home in Danzig. Documents confirm that he was the proprietor of a thriving, successful enterprise. In addition to the sawmill, on the same site there stood a parquet factory and a carpentry shop that made (among other things) paneling, desktops, and chairs. The warehouse was located at the compound of the Bergford Company at 9 Morska Street. Hil now belonged to the circle of Danzig wood exporters that traded with various European countries, especially Sweden through the Anton Karsksens Company.

Hil and Leo at the Gdynia sawmill

In October 2006, while in Israel, I had a conversation with my father's second cousin, Michael Garin (formerly Grunhaus) and learned much about my father's personality in those prewar years. Although Michael was some 15 to 18 years younger than Hil, he had a close relationship with his cousin. Michael came from Warsaw, where his father, Henryk Grunhaus (Yechiel Asher), made parquet flooring, door frames, and windows. Henryk had business dealings with Grandfather Jacob and with Hil, who would visit these Warsaw relatives on his monthly trips between Włodawa and Gdynia.

Michael had great admiration and respect for my father, feelings that lasted all his life. He would address him affectionately as Henryk, in Polish. Here is how he described the Hil of those years: "Picture this guy who was born in Włodawa, a provincial town, a 'hole,' and he comes to Warsaw. Handsome, elegant, and well-dressed. Cheerful, funny. Heavy smoker. Spoke perfect Polish. He enjoyed going out to have a good time. You would have thought he was born in Warsaw. A miracle." Michael's mother considered Hil such a good catch that when she heard he was coming to town, she would inform her five sisters so they could prepare. They did so by purchasing new outfits and visiting the beauty parlor. They would fight over who was going to go out with him. Hil would take them to movies, night clubs, and cafes – he was splendid. Michael's aunts loved being with him. He was most entertaining and everywhere they went he was the center of attention.

Michael also stressed how smart my father was. Hil was quite foresighted in deciding to establish an enterprise in Gdynia, a new city with a building boom that called for an immense amount of wood. He drew up a plan for an industrial complex so he could do business not just in Poland but to also export lumber and wood products to other European countries. Michael told us that early on they all realized Hil would be making a great deal of money with these new undertakings, and he did indeed. From the first year, his projects earned sizeable profits. Michael's father had great respect for Hil's views. Wanting Michael to eventually participate in the family dealings, his father would include the boy in his talks with Hil to help him learn how things worked.

What Michael valued most was the personal side of his relationship with Hil. "Henryk [Hil] was the one who turned my dreams into reality. Dear to so many people, he made me appreciate different ways of life. He also taught me values. I adored him." One memorable event occurred in 1937. Hil took Michael to Włodawa for his brother Leo's wedding. According to Michael's account, Leo was a tall, handsome fellow, and his bride, Bela Wacht – who was not from Włodawa – was so lovely and elegant that she greatly impressed the visiting cousin. But most of all, it was Grandfather Jacob's appearance that astonished him – the beard and the way he dressed were all in all the look of an extremely Orthodox Jew. Along with that, the family house seemed huge: "It had a gigantic kitchen. You could cook a meal for 100 people there."

Indeed, for Michael, coming to Włodawa was quite an amazing adventure, as if he had gone back in time 200 years. He remarked that all the stores belonged to Jews and that the farmers from the surrounding area came into town to shop. He must have been there on a market day. For someone from cosmopolitan Warsaw, Włodawa was something of a primitive place. Since he could not communicate with most of its inhabitants (he was a Polish speaker who knew no Yiddish), he made the mistake of concluding that – since the majority of Włodawa's Jews were religious – the city had no culture. Michael also commented on how much my father respected his parents.

In Warsaw, Hil primarily lived as a secular Jew, yet back home he participated in some religious practices and traditions. My guess is that Michael, his family, and his social circle, were quite liberal and that was why the Orthodox ways in Włodawa came as a surprise. The differences between Warsaw, the capital, and this little eastern Polish shtetl were enormous: the buildings, the religiosity, the garb of the Jews, the use of Yiddish rather than Polish. It was another world. Hil, however, was at ease in both environments, passing from one to the other without conflict and with a marvelous capacity for adaptation.

Michael also had a chance to visit Leo and Bela's new home, located in a three-story building, and saw that they had a rather secular lifestyle.

In a photo apparently taken in these quarters, we see Leo and Bela in the dining room, seated with Helena and David Widra and my father. The setting is strikingly ordinary: wooden furniture with simple, almost Nordic lines; framed landscapes on the wall; big lamp over the table; no reminders of religion. The women wear short-sleeved gowns, and the men are bareheaded, no *kippahs*. In another photo from 1938, we see Leo and Bela embracing or looking tenderly at their newborn daughter Pola (Pesa).

Leo, Bela, Helena, David and Hil

Leo, Bela and Pola

Michael spoke of my father as a cosmopolitan Jew who knew how to enjoy all the opportunities Warsaw had to offer. Hil went to both the Yiddish and Polish theaters, and to concerts, cabarets, lectures, and meetings. Indeed, in those years between the two wars he took advantage of any occasion that allowed him to forget for a while the antisemitism that had grown exponentially since the death of the Polish president, Marshal Józef Piłsudski, in 1935. When we would ask my father how noticeable antisemitism was in Poland, he would usually say, "If the economic situation was normal, Poles were friendly toward the Jews, when it worsened, one would start listening to the shouts directed at them. The Jew was repeatedly the one responsible."

In 1933 the Nazi Party won the elections in Danzig. Hil immediately moved to Gdynia and went on working. In 1937, a couple of years before the war started, he and his brother Leo started a company called "Grünhaus Wood, Warehousing, Processing, and Exporting." Their head office was at 58 Morska Street in Gdynia, according to the city's 1938 telephone directory. My father used to talk often about his brother Leo. It was obvious they had a strong and special connection, both personally and professionally.

Sara Omelinski (née Lustigman), who later became a close friend of my mother, confirmed that my father was a successful businessman. Even though Sara did not know my mother prior to the war, she was acquainted with my father and his family. On Saturday mornings Hil's mother, Rosa, often went to pray at the Lustigman's where there was a house of prayer. Since my father returned home for all the religious holidays, surely at some time he accompanied his mother to the Lustigman's for Saturday prayers. Sara knew him to have had several girlfriends as well – the last being Ida who was tall and worked as a private tutor.

On September 1, 1939, the Nazis invaded Poland. On September 14, they reached Gdynia. Immediately they seized my father's assets. At that, he made his way to Włodawa to be with his family.

7

LIFE DISRUPTED

On September 3, 1939, the Germans bombed Włodawa for the first time. They attacked the train station and destroyed the bridge over the Bug River which had connected Włodawa and Tomaszówka.

My mother was not yet 15 but I am sure many disturbing thoughts were going through her head. As sheltered as she was, she must have been alarmed, afraid, and aware that "the Poles were not prepared to confront the German war machine. The situation was critical: cavalry against tanks ... how were the Poles going to defend themselves?"

On September 17, the Soviet Union invaded from the east. Following the guidelines set out in the Molotov-Ribbentrop Pact, the Russians and the Germans shared Poland, dividing it into two parts. Hitler – carrying out his ambition to extend the boundaries of his country and create more *Lebensraum* (German living space) – annexed most of the north and west of Poland, the Warthegau. The central area, which included Warsaw and Włodawa, became an occupied zone known as the General Government (GG). Non-German peoples – Poles, Jews, and other groups – were driven out of the Warthegau into the GG.

Since Włodawa bordered the Soviet Union, the city filled up with Jewish and Polish refugees fleeing toward the east. Many crossed the

Bug, others stayed in Włodawa expecting the conflict would be short lived. The situation in the city turned chaotic. The mayor ordered stores to stay open during Rosh Hashanah, allowing people to stock up on provisions. Young Alexandra surely wondered what was going to happen, how they were going to be able to take in so many people, and what would become of them all.

On September 16 (according to some sources; others say it was the 17th or 18th), the Germans entered Włodawa. Random shootings and killings began, intended to spread terror. My mother told us that early on they took several hundred Jewish men prisoner and held them in the main synagogue, threatening to burn down the building with them inside. The captives were kept there without food or water. Shots were fired through the windows, wounding many. After 48 hours, once the ransom demanded by the Germans had been paid, most of the hostages were released, except for ten who endured beatings before finally being freed. Four days later (sometime between September 22 and 25, by varying accounts), German forces withdrew from Włodawa and advanced toward the west to allow for the incursion of Soviet troops. While this was occurring, Polish troops came in for a few days, led by General Kleeberg, but his forces abandoned the city on September 29, the day after Poland surrendered.

The Soviets occupied Włodawa for two weeks, from the end of September until October 10 (or 14, according to some sources). Their presence meant a brief respite. Right away they set up revolutionary committees and recognized all legal residents of the area as Soviet citizens. They offered refugees the option of becoming Soviet citizens or returning to their places of origin. Some Jews took advantage of the opportunity to flee German zones, moving into the areas under Soviet control. On October 10, the Germans and Russians signed a new agreement. In accordance with its terms the Soviets withdrew, inviting the population to join them but most people decided not to leave Poland, afraid of being separated from family.

As for Esther and my mother, they were not prepared to make such a decision as to leave Włodawa and cross the border without their family. Why their father – who later showed such common sense in his decisions – did not make his two unmarried daughters escape to Russia is unknown. But certainly, to do so would have required great fortitude on his part and more than a vague foreboding of what was to come.

With the Russians gone, the Germans returned, setting up a temporary German civil administration. Włodawa was incorporated into the municipality of Chelm in the Lublin District. On October 25, military and police forces came in – among them the Security Police (SiPo and SD) – to control the city, eliminating all civic participation. The Polish police and officials were evicted from their headquarters.

"The beginning of the war was terrible. Every day they required something different," my mother told us. First, they made the residents of the city create a *Judenrat* (Jewish Council) to administer and enforce German orders. Then, they set up a Jewish Order Service, which often had to deal with difficult tasks such as searching homes or rounding up Jews on the streets for various reasons.

Individuals were frequently targeted for execution. Any Jew could be seized and made to do forced labor. If he hesitated for even a moment, that would be enough for him to be shot dead. The first jobs consisted of repairing bomb damage, cleaning floors, cutting wood, and rebuilding the bridge over the Bug. "The Judenrat had to give the Germans all they requested. At first, that meant workers," my mother recalled. By overseeing the organization of the work projects, the members of the Judenrat believed they might be able to reduce the level of violence afflicting the city. But it did not happen that way, and the Germans continued to carry out daily raids. Any male between the ages of 12 and 60 could be recruited, so Jews avoided leaving their houses as much as possible. Religious men in particular were constantly subjected to acts of aggression: the Germans would pull on their beards or cut them off, all the while mocking their victims; they made them sing and dance in the street, humiliated them and broke their religious symbols. Alexandra and Esther must have certainly feared that their father and brother, Joseph, would be attacked or mistreated.

In November, Richard Nitschke arrived in Włodawa. He was a sub-lieutenant in the *SS* (Schutzstaffel), the Nazi regime's Special Forces, and had been named head of the Border Police. Attached to the *SD* (Sicherheitsdienst, the Security Service) in Lublin, Nitschke took on the duties of the *Gestapo* (the Secret State Police). According to descriptions, he was a short, fat man with blond hair, a round face, and was about 41 years old. He was responsible for Włodawa and the surrounding area until the end of 1942. Under Nitschke's influence, outrages against Jews increased. He would go out walking with a large dog, which he would incite to bite any Jew they encountered. My mother said, "People were terrified of that dog. It would kill for any little thing."

The first act of aggression aimed at a group occurred in November, leaving a deep impression on my mother, who observed, "They chose 30 people from Włodawa, the leaders, the wealthiest, took them to another city where they beat them until they passed out, swollen." The entire city saw how they looked upon their return; perhaps it was then that the Jews of Włodawa began to understand what was to come. My father and his brother Leo were among those detained.

My mother went on: "The laws started. Really bad laws." Each regulation was posted on the main square to inform the whole town. In November began the humiliation of having to wear a white armband with a blue star of David. Jewish schools were closed, and Jews were forbidden from attending the public schools. A curfew was in force from 9 p.m. to 5 a.m. Jews had to doff their hats before Germans and could not pass them on the street or use the sidewalks.

And my mother had more to add: "Then they asked for furs, money, jewelry ... We had to go around collecting things from people to give the Germans what they wanted." Jews found themselves obliged to provide the enemy with desirable items: clothes, coats, boots, household articles, furniture, food. They also had to pay ransom to get people released or to avoid reprisals. No one was allowed to change residence or move to another city without official approval. Soon Jews were forced to register their belongings and were not allowed to possess or buy gold or other metals. Financial restrictions put in place made it impossible to perform any kind of transaction, including barter. Early on, the Germans noted which stores were Jewish. Before long, these were closed or confiscated, then turned over to the Ukrainians. Many of the Jewish owners were forced to work in their own businesses as unpaid employees. The situation was the same with Jewish pharmacies, bookstores, libraries, and workshops. The many prohibitions and restrictive measures changed life for all. Any act of disobedience would be punished immediately with blows continuing until the victim fell to the ground unconscious.

November also saw the start of rationing. The Germans allotted three and a half ounces of bread per day, per person, which could only be purchased at one of the two bakeries still operating. Baking at home was not permitted. Only a small cooperative, not good for much, stayed open. In Włodawa, already a rather poor community, hunger increased, illness and death coming with it. From the start, the Germans had set out to drive the Jews into extreme poverty and soon succeeded in doing so. Even an adolescent like Alexandra understood their goal.

Early on, Włodawa was a place where Jews from surrounding areas concentrated. My mother used to talk about how many refugees there were. In December 1939 alone several hundred people arrived from Kalisz and other places, fleeing terrible situations in their towns. Overcrowding began to wreak havoc. Seeing the conditions of these new arrivals deeply affected my mother: "We were fine because we did not have to leave our homes, we were not refugees. We would be hungry, but the refugees suffered more than us; they were bloated from hunger."

When the Germans closed Grandfather Moses' shop, he was able to put away some merchandise, which he would sell on the black market so the family could survive. As time went on, to subsist he had to get rid of many other things: clothes, coats, furniture, all that was in the house. Alexandra's sister Esther was most daring: "When regulations were still not too strict, Esther used to go to a nearby city, Chelm, where she bought merchandise to bring back to Włodawa and sell." That helped for a while, until travel between cities was prohibited.

At that time, several German firms came to Włodawa and began using Jewish workers. The biggest employer was the Rhode Company, with a commission to channel the waters and drain the swamps. So that these tasks could be accomplished, an *Arbeitsamt* (employment office) was set up – dependent on the Judenrat – which handed out the jobs. The Judenrat had to provide between 500–1,000 people a day for forced labor. It drew up a daily list of "volunteers." Several of the work sites were outside of town, places where hundreds of laborers would dig ditches and fortify riverbeds. Working conditions were terrible: long hours standing in water in swamps and marshes. Many stayed away from the Arbeitsamt for fear of being recruited. People said the members of the Judenrat avoided assigning this type of labor to their relatives. Whenever Grandfather Moses was called in, some of his children showed up instead, which my mother did several times. She told us she never had to do anything too strenuous since she worked alongside German soldiers, who "were not as bad as the others." Cooking and cleaning for the Germans were also lighter tasks assigned to some women.

The Judenrat received money for supplying the workers they sent to some of the companies. Though it was not much, the funds helped provide food for Jews living in misery, who were under great pressure. Occasionally the Judenrat needed volunteers and that was how Esther, carrying out an assignment in a makeshift hospital, met Jehudit, a sister of Sara Omelinski. Through this connection, Sara and my mother came to know each other. It was the beginning of an extremely important friendship that developed when the two of them became survivors.

On September 10, 1940, Bernhard Falkenberg arrived in Włodawa. He was a German, contracted by the Rhode Company to direct the projects of regulating, channeling, and drying up lakes and marshes – and canalizing rivers and streams – ordered by the head of the Lublin Water Facilities Commission, Franz Holtzheimer. As a start, Falkenberg gave work to 180 Jews, and by 1942, he had 1,500–2,000 laborers, quite a few more than he really needed. Falkenberg realized from the beginning that the German objective was to exterminate the Jews. Subtly, quietly, he decided to try to help as many as he could – by working for him, they would get better food rations and official work permits. His employees gathered each morning on an empty lot next to his house at 8 Kraszewskiego Street, where they would pick up tools and walk to various work sites, as far as three, or even seven kilometers away.

The Falkenberg house during the war (Krysztof Skibinski)

A *Volksdeutsche*[1] from Łódź, a man named Antoniewicz, was assigned to Włodawa and put in charge of the forests in the area. Forty women worked under him doing light tasks such as planting and nurturing trees that would eventually be moved to the woods. Some were made to build fences, a job notably more difficult and strenuous. People looked on Antoniewicz as a fair boss. Still others found work at a sawmill, administered by a man named Lemanschik, a Volksdeutsche who had arrived in Włodawa from Gdynia.

During the first year of the hostilities, Alexandra had as a pupil a boy from a wealthy family, who came to her house to work on reading and writing in Polish. Then for at least another year, she held classes for ten or so small children, in which they learned to read and write. Fond of singing, she also entertained them. The youngsters put on a presentation, Alexandra teaching them the songs, Esther the dances. In a photo from the *Yizkor Book*, there is my mother, young and smiling broadly, garbed modestly in a long-sleeved, high-collared dress, standing next to nine of her students – boys and girls of various ages.

Alexandra with her pupils (Yizkor Book)

How the Germans used deceit constantly tormented my mother. Young as she was back then, she realized they "behaved according to a plan. At first, the Nazis lied so people would reason nothing was going to happen to them, and that meant they would not be aware of what was going on. It was terrible." And that is how it was in 1940 when the authorities organized a group called "sanitation workers." At first, these health aides would go through the streets, checking to see that everything was kept clean, that the fronts of houses looked tidy. But before long they were turned into police. My mother recalled that the Germans assigned many well-off people to this group: "Everybody had to work, and people figured that this would be a good job but when they were turned into police ... who would dare say 'I do not want to do that'? They could not refuse because the Germans were likely to kill them." Without fail, my mother spoke well of the Jewish police. For her they did not take part in abusive or aggressive acts. They were simply keeping watch as a means of having work. She considered them just like other Jews and did not want to pass judgment on anyone's choices in such difficult, critical times.

It became harder and harder to buy food since Jews could not do any kind of trade with Poles, including farmers, and people were forced to resort to the black market where they exchanged the little they had for flour, potatoes, and firewood. They could also shop in cooperatives run by the Judenrat. *Joint* (the American Jewish Joint Distribution Committee), a North American Jewish aid organization that was headquartered in New York, was able to send food to the cooperatives until 1941. After that, only matches, candles, and salt arrived. Occasionally the Germans would supply rotten potatoes and brown sugar.

Early in 1941, the Germans forced the Jews to move from the main street to another specified area. Neither my mother nor other survivors referred to this section of town as a ghetto but as the "Jewish zone." The evictions were abrupt: the police showed up and gave residents ten minutes to collect a few belongings before abandoning their homes. The majority relocated with family or friends. The house of my mother's family on Błotna Street lay just within the Jewish zone which encompassed several streets – Kozia, Solna (Czerwonego Krzyża today), Furmańska, Kotlarska, and Okunińska. The Włodawa ghetto came into existence much later, toward the end of 1942.

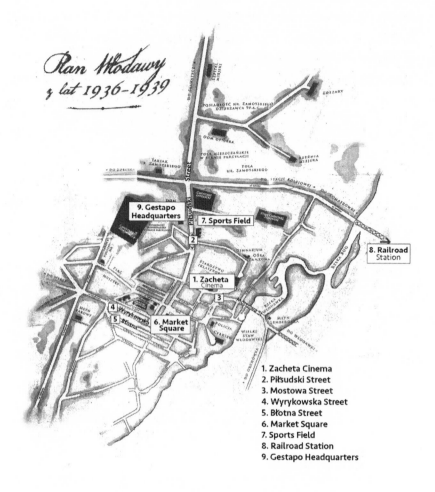

Plan Włodawy
z lat 1936–1939

9. Gestapo Headquarters

7. Sports Field

8. Railroad Station

1. Zacheta Cinema

6. Market Square

1. Zacheta Cinema
2. Piłsudski Street
3. Mostowa Street
4. Wyrykowska Street
5. Błotna Street
6. Market Square
7. Sports Field
8. Railroad Station
9. Gestapo Headquarters

It must have also been in 1941 that Alexandra, Esther, and Deborah started working for Antoniewicz who already employed Sara Omelinski and her two sisters. To get a legal work permit (and thus avoid being arrested) it was necessary to have an official occupation. Sometimes the work did not turn out to be heavy, although my mother still looked back on it as most definitely "slave labor, done from morning to night, with scant pay, not enough to eat on."

In June 1941, Germany declared war on the Soviet Union. For three or four months the repressive measures decreased because the military offensive kept the Germans busy. The situation for the Jews did not improve. Five hundred refugees arrived from Krakow, which complicated the food and health situation, leading to an outbreak of typhus. Miraculously, the infectious spread was kept under control: of the 102 who fell ill, only one died.

After that, according to my mother, "Living only got more and more difficult, all of us in great fear. For any infraction of their laws, the Germans killed; they sought out lawbreakers and murdered them. They went about with dogs and were constantly doing house searches. If a Jew out in the town had a beard, the Germans would cut it off with a knife." In 1942, when the owning of furs of any sort was banned, some tried to keep theirs hidden even under the menace of death; others preferred to burn them, but anyone discovered doing such things was executed.

In early 1942, the Judenrat discovered that the roundups were to begin. Through Falkenberg, the Jewish community mobilized and collected a bribe of six-and-a-half pounds of gold in one-dollar coins (90 coins), thus postponing for a few months the kind of operations that had already started taking place in other cities in the Lublin district. But the situation worsened in April with the arrival of 1,000 Jews from Vienna. With great effort and some help from Falkenberg, the city managed to find lodging for some of them in Jewish homes and to provide work for 300. The rest were left out on the street. One of the things that most impacted my mother about these unfortunate refugees was that "many of them did not even suspect that they were Jewish. Perhaps one of their grandparents had been. They came with their suitcases, elegant ones. Włodawa could not supply housing for so many arrivals. When people were removed from their homes, it meant they would likely die, for there was no one they could turn to, nor could they find anything to eat. The suffering was intense."

In April, two men – naked and traumatized – arrived in Włodawa. They had been among 150 workers sent to do construction at Sobibor back in March.[2] They said the project from which they managed to escape involved building so-called "baths," which in truth were gas chambers that prisoners would enter but not leave. Nobody believed their story. But Shmuel Shlomo Leiner, the Radzyń rabbi (who had been living in Włodawa since 1939), knew the men were telling the truth and understood exactly what was happening. Through his followers, the courageous rabbi urged young people to take up armed resistance and flee to the woods to save themselves. He also ordered a three-day fast to protest the construction taking place in Sobibor. Since it was extremely difficult to escape at that time, many chose to obey him by fasting, including Grandfather Moses and Joseph. The Germans heard about this activity through two Jewish informants and interpreted the fast as a rebellion. They sent a Jewish policeman named Moszko Minc to arrest the rabbi, even as his followers begged the officer to let him go; Minc refused out of fear for his family. With the help of the Judenrat, there was an attempt to bribe the Gestapo, giving them gold and jewels. Nitschke offered to let him go free. In the end, however, that did not happen, and the Germans sent the rabbi to the work camp in Tomaszówka for a week. On May 16, he was brought back to Włodawa where he was murdered in the Jewish cemetery. Later people learned the Nazis had found him there wrapped in his father's *tallit*. When one of the officers gave him an aggressive shove, the rabbi had the courage to turn around and slap the man before being executed. The rabbi's followers stabbed the Jewish policeman responsible for the original arrest, yet the wounds were not fatal.

One of the most upsetting events for the Jews of Włodawa took place in the spring of 1942. The Germans decided to widen Solna Street down to Musztry Square and they forced the Jewish workmen to use gravestones as building material. Weeping and begging the forgiveness of the dead for profaning their graves, the laborers were obliged to carry out the order. This incident was emotionally devastating, especially for anyone who came across the tomb of a friend or relative. And that is what happened to David Holzmann, who, upon locating his father's headstone, decided to lift it up himself amid shouts of despair, at the end reciting the prayers for the dead.[3]

Jews continued arriving from other towns, cities, and countries –
from Mielec, Radzyń, and Vienna. Włodawa had been turned into a
Judenstadt – a city for concentrating Jews. The Judenrat, desperate,
finally got help from the Jewish Cooperative of Krakow through
Chelm. A branch was established in Włodawa to provide food and
medical supplies for the displaced, such aid lasting until October
1942. The office received provisions for the communal kitchen, but
the daily bread allotment was decreased to less than three ounces per
person.

8

IN CONSTANT PERIL

The Germans entered Gdynia on September 14, 1939. Anti-Jewish rules and attacks began immediately. They arrested my father, Hil Grunhaus, and after writing up a report, released him. He then had to turn his business and his house over to Verner Wege and Brunon Seidel, Danzig citizens authorized to confiscate Jewish property. My father told us how he simply handed over the keys and left when the new owners arrived. The picture was somewhat more positive when it came to his sawmill. The Germans chose a Volksdeutsche named Lemanschik to run it. He had worked with Hil in the past and since the two were good friends, once taking over he agreed to continue sharing the profits.

In November, Hil returned to Włodawa. The trip from Gdynia to Włodawa was long and disheartening. He saw how the Germans were treating the Polish population and the Jews in the cities he passed through; Anti-Jewish propaganda was everywhere. The Germans posted signs in public places that depicted Jews in degrading ways, with text that referred to them as worms, vermin, or dirty creatures, and blamed them for the war.

In Włodawa, Nitschke had set up his headquarters by appropriating the tax collection office – Dom Urzédników – which stood on

Piłsudskiego Street, across from the playing field. The SS and the Gestapo had taken charge of civilian government, confiscating several buildings for their own use, among them the main synagogue which became a military warehouse.

Right away Hil, himself, was subjected to the physical violence that would characterize the entire period of the Occupation. The last week in November members of the Gestapo arrived to arrest him. He was living at his parents' house. His brother Leo was also apprehended. They detained a total of 31 men between the ages of 30 and 70, all of them prominent citizens. At Gestapo headquarters, their belongings were taken. Then, without explanation, each detainee was handed back 20 złotys. For several hours the men had to chop wood and carry water until, totally exhausted, they were transported to Chelm in a covered vehicle. At the Chelm police station, they climbed out amid whiplashes and were jammed into two cells. Then the Gestapo called them out one by one, returning them to their cells brutally beaten and close to passing out.

My father later gave a detailed account of what happened:

> They took me into a large room where there were about ten individuals from the Gestapo with [their] sleeves rolled up. There was a table and some chairs. A faint light illuminated the walls where torture instruments were hung, and I was ordered to undress completely. While punishing me they kept asking me stupid political questions, paying no attention to the answers. They covered my face with a gas mask, laid me down on the table and gave me a series of lashes. I do not recall how long this lasted. I only remember the beginning because I passed out. Then I realized I was being dressed and hit at the same time and passed out again. I woke up in the hallway and, semiconscious, as if through a haze I saw my brother being brought out and placed next to me. That revived me completely and I began to bring him to. The guard let the two of us go out on the prison patio for a little fresh air. We did not get a drop of water. We were all thrown back into one of the two cells. We were not hungry, just dying of thirst. The younger prisoners, including

59

me, held up pretty well. The older ones, who were barely conscious, hardly knew what they were doing or saying.

After midday, the Germans set us free and ordered us to go to the train station and buy tickets for Włodawa. Then we realized why they had left us each 20 złotys – just enough for the fare back home. We were all in a deplorable state. We had to form a double line and were more or less dragged through the streets to the station. None of us really had the strength to walk a few kilometers, we forced ourselves to because we were going home. Most of us had disfigured faces. Leo and I had been spared because of the gas masks they had put on our faces. At the Bug Station, the SS was waiting with horses and wagons, and they made us unload the train, which was bringing six cars full of heavy freight – cement and building materials. Then we were shoved into the wagons for the ride to town Since it was already dark and Shabbat had begun, those who could got out, walking to the city so as not to profane the sanctity of the holy day.

In Włodawa many were waiting for them since the Judenrat had been informed. They had already paid the 50,000 złotys demanded as ransom. First the men were taken to the Gestapo offices where Nitschke greeted them and explained they were hostages who would be held responsible for anything that might happen to any German. Upon which he ordered them to return to their homes "serenely and heroically." It took many months to recover from the blows received, the younger victims came back to good health but many of the older ones never recovered fully.

In December another incident shocked the city: 320 Jewish soldiers from the Polish army, having fallen into German hands, arrived in the wooded area near Sobibor. They were prisoners of war – POWs – whom the Germans had separated from the other POWs, sending them to eastern Poland in closed train cars usually used to transport livestock. It was a seven-day journey with no food or water. During the trip, many died of cold or starvation. The survivors had to get off the train at the Bug-Włodawski Station and walk to the forest carrying the dead and wounded. Once there, the Germans shot them.

A few escaped and arrived in Włodawa in grave condition. The Judenrat took charge of the situation, paying a ransom to the Germans so the dead could be buried once the bodies had been identified. Rabbi Menahem Mendl Morgenstern supervised the process according to Jewish rite, and Hil Grunhaus assisted him in the terrible task of making up a list of the deceased to take to the Warsaw Judenrat so the news could be passed on to family members.

The community set up a center in two houses on Błotna Street to care for the wounded, since Jews were not allowed to use the Polish hospital. A Jewish physician named Dr. Springer, took charge of logistics and treatment. Some young Jewish women volunteered to serve as nurses, among them Esther and a sister of Sara Omelinski. Community solidarity was very much in force. "All Jews tried to help their fellows, their possibilities being quite limited," my father told us.

Like my mother, my father witnessed the various decrees and restrictive measures affecting Jews, and he was aware of several executions that had taken place when individuals were caught breaking the rules. Among the incidents he recalled was the case of the son and son-in-law of a certain Baruj Shalom. The two men were caught buying flour from a farmer and "as punishment, in that harsh winter they had to make two holes on the frozen surface of the Bug River and were then submerged in the openings until they died in the frigid water."

In early 1940, Hil went to Warsaw for a couple of months. Because he knew the wood trade, through a friend he obtained a special classification as an industrialist and became involved in laying out and installing tracks for the city's streetcar lines. That allowed him to earn some money and get a pass for travel between Warsaw and Włodawa. At Purim, he returned to Włodawa where he was arrested again along with his brother Leo. Fortunately, this time they suffered no physical harm, being released a few days later after paying a ransom of two pairs of high boots and some men's clothing.

We do not understand why Hil's father moved to another city once the war started. Maybe his parents hoped that by doing so one of them might survive. Hil's father, Jacob, went to Kovel where his younger daughter, Lola, had settled with her husband. The mother, Rosa, stayed in Włodawa with Hil and Leo. Kovel was under Soviet control until June 1941; then the Germans came in. Helena, the older daughter, may have also been in Kovel, or possibly in Białystok. What is certain is that all these family members met their deaths during one roundup or another. To protect his mother, Hil remained with her until the last possible moment. He had decided not to flee but to be there for his family, especially Rosa and Leo, and although he may not have said it, we suppose because of his girlfriend, Ida.

When war broke out, Hil was 35. He was familiar with several cities – Włodawa, Warsaw, Chelm, Lublin, Gdynia, and Danzig – spoke perfect Polish and knew how to move in non-Jewish surroundings. He traveled quite often, and while doing so, kept the armband identifying him as a Jew in his pocket. He took a lot of chances, was clever and confident, and when faced with difficult moments he reacted decisively. Thanks to the pass, Hil went on working and traveling until May 1942. It has been documented that such travel permits were handed out in the Lublin district. Because Hil had one, and because he was able to communicate with different members of the Judenrat, he acted as an emissary in various capacities: for example, in efforts to help secure the freedom of imprisoned individuals or simply to bring messages to the Warsaw Judenrat.

In May 1940, Hil's friend Lemanschik arrived from Gdynia to run the Włodawa sawmill. Since the family sawmill was in Tomaszówka and that town was held by the Soviets, Hil saw to it that his brother, Leo, was assigned to the one in Włodawa along with 20 other Jewish men. Thanks to the three employers – Falkenberg, Antoniewicz, and Lemanschik – many Włodawa Jews lived in relative tranquility because they had work permits and received decent treatment and adequate food rations. In addition, they were not confined in a work camp. It was probably through Lemanschik that Hil ended up becoming close friends with Falkenberg. Hil understood from the start that this was an atypical German, someone who got along well with Jews. The 2,000 or so individuals Falkenberg kept employed could consider themselves privileged. Their workdays were long and hard, but Falkenberg took an interest in their well-being and above all in their safety. To achieve this, he counted on help from Holtzheimer, from whom he received his orders. Falkenberg protected them in any way he could and warned them about upcoming roundups. He went so far as to hide Jews on his property. Hil was in constant communication with him, sometimes getting Falkenberg to hire people he knew – which was made easier because Falkenberg had good relations with the Germans as well as the Judenrat, both sides trusting the man.

In 1940, when the Germans created the sanitary worker crews, Hil was offered the job as commander of the local brigade but he refused categorically, so another Jew was brought from Chelm to fill the position. At first, many young people – among them some Hasidic Jews – desired employment as sanitary police, anticipating that would contribute to their security, but time proved them wrong. The sanitary workers not only had to deal with harsh tasks such as taking Jews from their homes and arresting them during roundups but also found they were looked down on by many, who claimed that "any job was better than that of [a] policeman."

Jews tried insofar as possible to hold on to their religious practices and celebrate their holidays. For the *Sukkoth* in October 1940, a friend from Italy sent Hil *etrog and lulav* (bitter lemon with a bouquet of palm fronds plus willow and myrtle boughs), and he brought a few to Włodawa to help people there observe the festival as they had before the war. The rest of that year passed in relative calm, with only a few isolated incidents of a serious kind. People held the vain hope that the situation would change. "We had faith in God and the civilized world," my father wrote later.

Starting in 1941 the situation grew more dangerous each day. Executions increased and any transgression, no matter how minor, was punished by death. My father told us how the Germans arrested a group of Poles that year, mostly from the professional and intellectual classes, sending them first to Schloss Prison in Lublin and then to Auschwitz. He himself was arrested in April and Nitschke personally escorted him to Schloss where he ran into these Polish prisoners and observed the weekly departures to Auschwitz. The Nazis murdered many of them, sending their remains to their families in urns accompanied by a certificate stating the cause of death as heart attack. As for Hil, they finally released him on June 21, 1941, after 79 days of incarceration, and only because his family had paid a sizeable ransom.

My mother commented that after the war broke out between Germany and the Soviet Union (which happened on June 27) atrocities decreased, and the Jews had a brief respite. And in Warsaw, too, things calmed down. In my father's words, "The Jews were working and once again putting their hope in God." The various Judenrats were active, doing all they could to help the ailing and the needy.

In 1942 conditions in the various cities in the General Government rapidly deteriorated and roundups soon began. Since Hil ran a risk by traveling back and forth, he returned to Włodawa for good. En route, for the first time he heard rumors about the existence of Sobibor. As the train got closer, he heard Polish passengers talking about the horrific events at that concentration camp. Years later he remembered his reaction to the distressing talk: "I thought such barbarism is impossible in the 20th century; Germany will not dare commit that kind of barbarity. I refuse to accept it; I cannot accept it. ... Right then I resolved not sit idly by. I had to do something."

On Tuesday, May 19, the chairman of the Włodawa Judenrat contacted Hil and asked for help in the face of "a grave situation affecting the Jewish residents of the city." Three members of the Chelm District SA (Sturmabteilung, a Nazi paramilitary organization also known as Stormtroopers or Brownshirts) had arrived in Włodawa and ordered the Judenrat to hand over 3,000 Jews who were to be sent to work camps. The Judenrat had managed to lower this number to 1,500 in exchange for a large amount of gold. They asked Hil to go Chelm to negotiate the change in the order and consult with the local Judenrat there about how to proceed. Apprehensive about the responsibility and the fact that he did not belong to the Judenrat, Hil agreed to go but insisted that one of its members accompany him. A member named Mr. Branschteter was chosen to serve as the official representative and be Hil's traveling companion, and a member of the Polish Command was also an escort. The Gestapo granted a special pass to the three men, and they boarded a train on the morning of Wednesday, May 20. In Chelm they learned that a roundup was underway and were warned not to enter the main part of town. They exercised caution but encountered nothing – in fact, the streets were deserted. There was no one to be found, not even the local Judenrat, so no arrangement could be made for the Jews in Włodawa. The three men traveled back home with the bad news.

9

FEAR, DEATH, AND DESTRUCTION (ALEXANDRA'S STORY)

Between May 22 and May 24 during *Shavuot,* Włodawa endured its first *Aktzia* (the Polish name for the Nazi roundups of Jews). My mother remembered how on Thursday, May 21, the loudspeakers began summoning the Jewish refugees from Vienna, as well as the ailing, disabled, and older people, supposedly to "relocate" them. The Germans had ordered the Judenrat to collect 3,000 people. Since many were suspicious, only 1,500 showed up, most of them Viennese Jews who had obeyed the order. Those who did not appear were detained at random on the streets, with help from the Jewish Order Service. All ended up gathered in the market square and were then taken to a local movie theatre, the Zacheta. To prevent them from escaping, Nitschke had the exits blocked by a group of local officials – Müller, Schaub, Horna, Schwab, and Knippel. During the night, the Germans fired into the theatre and threw in grenades. Locked inside for two days, badly wounded, and with no food or water, few survived.

Since they had not managed to collect the total number of Jews they wanted, on May 24 the Germans went hunting through streets and houses, murdering many Jews, arresting others, and taking anyone who did not have a work permit. Then they led them and the few survivors from the movie theatre down Mostowa Street and along the Bug River to the Orchówek Station, about four kilometers from Włodawa. The sick and wounded traveled in carts or cattle wagons. At the station, they all climbed into a freight train headed for Sobibor. It has been said there were 1,300 people transported that day, 700 of them Jews from Vienna. Not one survived.

Motel Rabinowicz, a Włodawa survivor who entered the movie house after these events, described a terrifying scene: "The walls were covered with blood and everywhere there were pieces of bodies blown apart by grenades. The road to the train station was littered with household goods left behind, mostly by the Viennese Jews."

That first Aktzia marked the beginning of the mass annihilation of the Jews of Włodawa. Those who had not believed the escapees from Sobibor or who did not trust Rabbi Leiner's advice to flee or hide quickly realized they would never again hear news of the "relocated." After that, whenever special SS contingents started arriving in Włodawa, it was obvious another roundup was imminent.

My mother recalled that at home they were continually talking about "how awful the situation was." When someone from another city would arrive and enumerate the vicious acts – the outrages, the murders – it was hard to accept, people did not give credit to their words. "There was no way out, we could not help ourselves or save ourselves; we too were lost." If I asked her why they had not fled Włodawa after the first roundup, when it was already quite clear that the German objective was the liquidation of the Jews, she would answer: "Where could we go?" Back then, she was young, barely 18, and while she spoke perfect Polish, she had grown up immersed in a Hasidic world. Perhaps she could have tried to escape but she was timid and, more important, she was used to others, her father and Esther, making decisions for her. For the moment, although Włodawa was under German control, the city did not have a closed ghetto, and yet escape represented an extremely dangerous alternative. It would have required great daring to leave one's family and risk not finding any help in the Aryan world.

As the acts of extermination increased in the concentration camps, and the German objectives became more apparent, those who understood what was going on made various efforts to warn Polish Jews so they could take preventive measures. After the first roundup in Włodawa, an anonymous letter in Yiddish was written, dated June 1, 1942, which is now in the Oneg Shabbat archives in Warsaw.[1] Here is an excerpt:

> My uncle plans to celebrate his daughter's wedding in your midst also. He has rented a house near you, very near you. You probably did not have any idea this has happened. We are writing to make you aware of this so you will find a house outside the city, for you and your relatives and children since my uncle has already gotten a new house ready for all, the same as in our case.[2]

In cryptic language the letter was transmitting and stressing an essential message: "Flee Warsaw, hide, because the Germans are planning to kill all of you, just as happened to our loved ones."

At the end of July, the Germans posted notices in the rynek asking Jews to bring children under 14 years of age to the sports field. These announcements were generally disobeyed, with few showing up. Those who did were greeted by Nitschke and some aides who proceeded to examine the necks, eyes, and ears of all the children, leading parents to believe they were there for a physical exam. All were then released, feeling reassured. A couple of weeks later, on August 7, the Germans issued a new call and this time many more came. Seemingly they would be offering ration books to those making an appearance. Because of that, many parents dressed up their children, hoping to gain compassion from members of the Gestapo. Once the Jews were at the field, the Germans ordered the adults to leave. When the parents refused, they were cruelly and violently separated from the group of 107 children, whom the Gestapo proceeded to pile into wagons for the trip to Sobibor. Nitschke, Müller, and Shaub personally directed this Aktzia.

My Aunt Deborah and her family perished in this roundup, named the Children's Aktzia. On that occasion, the police were searching actively, so she hid inside the house with her two little ones – four-year-old Perla, and Nissim, who was one. The boy started to cry, was heard, and my aunt had to come out with the children. Officers detained them and took them to the sports field. They told Deborah the call was not for her, but she refused to leave. Her husband, Ruwin, who was working four kilometers away, received word of what was going on in Włodawa. He ran back home and headed to the field where his wife and two children had been detained. When trying to join the group, he was held back. After bribing the Ukrainian guard with his watch, Ruwin was allowed to accompany his family. All of them died at Sobibor. My mother told us this story, asking sorrowfully, "How was she going to leave the children?"

Rabbi Menahem Mendl Morgenstern, a public figure well known to the Germans, realized he could not hide nor hide his children, choosing to appear with them. There is a story that he and his wife tossed a coin to decide which one would accompany the youngsters, and when the Germans saw that the task had fallen to the rabbi, they offered to spare him. His refusal was firm and proud. "No, I am not going back. I shall accompany my children and all the city's children," he announced.

My mother told us she was never in danger during any of the roundups. Her father, Moses Aron, did not allow his children to appear any time there was a summons. "You have to stay out of sight," he would say. Accordingly, his youngest children – 13-year-old Abraham, and four-year-old Chava Rivka – did not go the sports field.

After this second Aktzia, the Germans ordered the Jews from neighboring towns to gather in Włodawa. Due to this, some distant relatives of the Ledermans arrived on their doorstep. There were already a considerable number of people in the house, but they had to receive their own family. The city was small, and the Jews were clustered on a few streets. There ended up being close to 10,000 of them, with up to 15 people living in a single room while many others were homeless. The Judenrat lacked the resources to provide shelter, food, or medical care. The situation was horrifying. "We were alone, on an island .... They brought more people, leaving them on the streets until they became swollen from hunger or came down with typhus or dysentery, waiting for a piece of bread or for their salvation through death, meanwhile becoming living corpses, incapable of thinking, morally and physically destroyed," stated Motel Rabinowicz in his testimony.

On Saturday, October 24, the Great Aktzia or Black Shabbat occurred. Additional forces, which had arrived the previous night, surrounded the city. There were so many Jews in Włodawa that reinforcements were called in, including the SD, the Polish police, the *Schutzpolizei* (uniformed police), the Ukrainians, and extra troops from the Chelm SS. Nitschke personally directed these forces.

That day it was pouring. Quite early, from my mother's house they heard the loudspeakers calling people to assemble at the sports field. After hiding their father, his wife, their younger siblings, and Joseph and his family in the store, my mother and Esther could not decide what to do. The two sisters were sure it was not a good idea to obey the order and became increasingly hesitant as everyone headed toward the field. The Christian wife of a Jewish policeman, their neighbor across the street, stood outside watching. The girls asked her opinion. In no uncertain terms, the woman said, "Hide. Do not go." Same as the advice from their father. A little shelter had been prepared by putting up a double wall in a small storage room in the entryway of their house. Now they shut themselves inside and waited. By the time of this roundup, many were living on the streets. Unable to stay out of sight, they voluntarily obeyed the summons. Young people hoped their work permits would save them. So many complied that the Germans did not bother to search as many houses as usual. The two girls were not discovered. Remaining in the shelter all day, they came out only after nightfall, when everybody had been taken away.

The sisters were not eyewitnesses to the brutal attacks of that day, but they did they hear the shouts, the wailing, the barking of the dogs, and the shots fired by the executioners. Sara Omelinski, my mother's friend, was at the sports field but escaped somehow, and in later years would recount the horrors she witnessed: "Upon arrival at the station, the men were separated from the women and the Germans tried to separate the mothers from the children. I lack words to describe what was happening. They were attacking the women with clubs, revolvers, and daggers, and the mothers would not let go of the little ones in their arms. Many of them assaulted the Germans like wounded tigers while trying to clutch their children more tightly. The cries and howls reached the heavens."[3]

My mother had not met Falkenberg herself, even though she heard what people said about him: "He was good because he fought to the last moment so they would let him work." And that was how he saved many. She found out that after the roundup he had hurried to the station to try to get his workers away. Apparently, he knew what was going to happen and hoped his employees might be spared. He had warned them and summoned them to come work at 3 a.m., saying that if they saw vehicles approaching, they should flee to the woods. The plan could not be carried out because Nitschke phoned the day before, ordering Falkenberg not to send any Jews out to work before he arrived. Nitschke showed up very early at the granary run by Falkenberg, who then tried to negotiate on behalf of his people, to no avail. They were made to line up by threes and proceed to the sports field.

Meanwhile, Falkenberg spoke to his superior, Holtzheimer, and told him what had happened. Holtzheimer then tried to intercede for the workers but the SS, which was in charge, did not give in. Seeing that he was getting nowhere, he ran to Falkenberg's house and phoned Lublin to speak directly to Globonick, the head of the GG police force, explaining how Jewish workers were necessary for ongoing projects. Globonick agreed he could take back 500 people. Based on that reply, Holtzheimer sent Falkenberg to the station. All the same, the command called Lublin for corroboration of the order. Finally,

400 individuals with work permits were allowed to get off the train. They became the first recruits in the Falkenberg *Lager,* or labor camp, set up between Wyrykowska and Kotlarska Street, with Błotna Street running down the middle. For the Jews who survived this last roundup in hiding, the Germans marked out a ghetto on the other side of the rynek, with Jatkowa Street in the center.

Falkenberg's workers joined the labor camp, as did those from the sawmill, like Hil and Leo, and Antoniewicz's employees, who included Alexandra, Esther, Sara, and her sisters. They all received work permits and wore numbers for control purposes. Nevertheless, in one way or another, 200 more friends and relatives were sneaked into the Lager. To prevent being discovered during the count, numbers were duplicated. Each person was assigned to a house where there could be four or five sleeping in one room. Only young, unmarried people were accepted. Esther and Alexandra remained in their home on Błotna Street, while Moses and Joseph and their families, without work permits, moved to the ghetto. Both the Lager and the ghetto had barbed wire fences but remained accessible.

Now the Lederman house had ten people living in its three rooms, two to a bed. Alexandra and Esther slept in one room; Yeshie and Leibe, maternal uncles who had lost their wives, bunked together; the rest shared the third room.

On November 7, Falkenberg's crews did not go to their worksites, suspecting another roundup was imminent. Indeed, a fourth one did take place, only in the ghetto. As usual, the Germans ordered the Jews to congregate in the market square. Many who did not have permission to reside in Włodawa remained hidden, afraid they would be selected. Intensive house-to-house searches took place over three days, with the breaking down of walls, the raising of floors, and the smashing of attics. Nitschke, accompanied by his dog, went around examining work permits. During an inspection at Falkenberg's camp, the Gestapo checked out the workers one by one, but each person's jacket bore a number and a badge, and no one was arrested. The officers went through the ghetto in hot pursuit, shooting many Jews –

probably close to 300. Bodies lay everywhere. Falkenberg's workers had to collect the dead, take them to the cemetery, and bury them. At the train station, since there was not enough room for all the prisoners, the guards ordered groups of seven or eight Jews to lie face down on the floor, then executed group after group. In this way they ended up killing 84 more people. Members of the Judenrat and the Jewish Police, along with 800 or more other Jews, were sent to Sobibor. Some people escaped discovery, including Moses Aron, Joseph, and their families.

Alexandra had a work permit with her real name, yet in November she obtained from a Polish woman the baptismal certificate of a deceased niece. We do not know how or why she did this while still living in Włodawa. Perhaps she had in mind that a false name would be necessary for escape, backed up by an official legal document. The paper was a certification from the Russian Orthodox Church, dated November 4, 1942, declaring that Alexandra Charkiewitsch, daughter of Stephan and Julie Weissruthenin, was born in Lewkovo (a village in northeast Poland), on October 3, 1922. From this document, Chana Szejndla (her birth name) took the name Alexandra that she would use the rest of her life.

At the end of October, a decree had been issued stating that Jews could only reside in one of eight specified cities, and only in a "Jewish residential zone" or *Judenwohnbezirk*. Włodawa was one of the cities. Once again, the Germans were being deceitful, assuring people there would be no more roundups, and once again, the Jews took them at their word. Thus, after the fourth Aktzia, the Włodawa ghetto filled up with Jews from Mielic, Kalisz, Radzyń, and other towns. By 1943, some 2,000 Jews were living in the ghetto and 500 in Falkenberg's camp. Conditions in the ghetto became desperate. Food was in short supply.

Also occurring that fall, a young man named Moshe Lichtenberg, whose wife and children had been murdered, fled Włodawa with 15 others to form a partisan group (one of several in the area). At first the group was located at Adampol, but it soon established a base in the woods. There, the members got themselves organized. The group's aim was to secure weapons for attacking the Germans. They started with an old rifle and an ancient revolver. A first cousin of Alexandra's, Yankel Lederman, and brothers Efraim and Srulke Fishman were among those who joined. These young people visited the city regularly to recruit members and visit relatives. Their ranks kept growing. These were the partisans of Włodawa.

The Lager and the ghetto stood on either side of the rynek. In Falkenberg's camp, conditions were slightly better than elsewhere, and everyone wanted to be there. At all costs, the Germans wished to prevent Jewish adults and children from hiding out in the Lager and decided to teach them a lesson. They called the workers together and a young fellow from Kalish was selected and forced to step out of the ranks. They accused him of having broken into a house, an excuse invented to kill him with a bullet in the back, terrifying all those present.

In the mornings the Ukrainians would come to collect the crew, opening the Lager gates, making a count, and then taking them by wagon to a worksite about four kilometers away. The days were 12 hours long, from 7 a.m. to 7 p.m. The going was hard, but Falkenberg was a good boss, as was Antoniewicz; however, unlike Falkenberg, he never tried to save or protect Jews on a large scale. At one point, he did announce to Alexandra, Esther, Sara, and her sisters that he had convinced a Polish farmers' family to take in one of them, provided the chosen one would learn Christian customs to pass as Polish. The girls decided the lucky one was to be Sara since she had green eyes. But when the Great Roundup took place Antoniewicz was out of town. After his return, the subject of such an arrangement never came up again, and the opportunity was lost.

Things calmed down for the time being. Some of Falkenberg's employees imagined that since their work was essential, they might be spared. Others thought that the German maneuver of letting Jews take refuge in Włodawa was aimed at keeping them concentrated in one place to make it easier to eventually wipe them out. Alexandra and Esther felt the end was coming and that they should act to save themselves. Since it was impossible to flee, their best chance for survival was to construct a secure hiding place.

There was still some communication with people in the ghetto. My mother told us how her father brought flour that Esther used for making bread to sell, which allowed them to get horsemeat and frozen potatoes. Some Jews were still trying to keep *kosher* – going hungry rather than eating non-kosher meat – though this occurred less with those living in the ghetto, especially families with children. My mother used to tell us: "I was young, and I had no children, so I did not brood about it a lot – what was going to happen to everyone else was going to happen to me. When you are young you don't fret all that much. Besides, I was lucky, very lucky, I never came face to face with death in a situation where I was up against Germans trying to kill me. I was fortunate because that never happened to me."

On the other hand, they were young and yearned to keep on living no matter what. Sara, my mother's best friend, described a party held in the ghetto on December 31, 1942. My mother's cousin, Yankel Lederman, went to pick up the girls at the Lager. Getting them out was not a problem since they had bribed the Ukrainian guard beforehand. "There was food such as we had not seen since before the war, and drinks too," Sara recalled. In the ghetto they ate, sang, and danced until another Ukrainian guard came in to see what was happening. They gave him so much vodka he got drunk and let them go on celebrating. At the end they all sang the "Hatikvah" – the Israeli national anthem. I have no idea whether Alexandra and Esther were present, nevertheless this event shows how the young people longed for a bit of emotional normality even for a few hours.

Time was passing and at the end of April 1943, Antoniewicz told his workers about the uprising in the Warsaw Ghetto. He was convinced the Germans would try to eliminate all the Jews before rumors of that rebellion could spread, inciting others to revolt. He was right.

Just after Passover, on April 30, heavily armed German soldiers surrounded the city. Accompanying them was a large contingent of *askaris*,[4] brought in to act as reinforcements during roundups, as they were crueler than the Germans. Many of them had dogs, which, upon hearing the word *Jude* (Jew) would leap on the chosen victim.

Early on the morning of Saturday, May 1, people heard a commotion in the streets and realized a fifth Aktzia was underway. Nitschke himself was no longer in Włodawa, having been transferred some 150 kilometers away to Kazimierz Dolny at the end of 1942. Under the direction of the Chelm Gendarmerie, security forces penetrated the ghetto and Falkenberg's camp simultaneously. They started a house-to-house search, forcibly removing the Jews they found, making them go to the sports field. Those who had hiding places prepared took refuge in them. The forces shot many people on the street, while others managed to escape into the woods. It is estimated that at the time there were approximately 2,000 Jews left in the ghetto and 500 to 700 in Falkenberg's camp. The exact number killed during this extermination action is unknown. From May 12 to May 13, the Germans again searched all the houses in town and found 300 more Jews, whom they sent to Sobibor. Now Włodawa was considered *Judenrein* – that is, cleansed of Jews.

Even with this exhaustive search, some were not discovered. The Lederman family house had a small cellar that some friends – Yehezkel Huberman and others – had spent weeks enlarging. On the kitchen floor, in front of the stove was a large metal plate that had been installed to guard against fires. Someone had the idea of digging under it at night. Disposing of the rubble proved tricky but all the same it was done. The project was not too difficult since the Ukrainians guarding the camp only opened the gates in the morning to count the residents, leaving them in peace at night and on holidays. The diggers fashioned a double roof to muffle noise and echoes so that anyone pounding on the floor would not hear a hollow sound. They put in a ladder for climbing down, added some wooden benches, and the bunker was ready.

The day the roundup began, Esther baked bread because Passover had ended. When those in the house realized the Aktzia was underway, they immediately collected bread, butter, and water and climbed into the basement which filled up fast. Yehezkel Huberman went to get Sara and her sisters. People were desperate, with nowhere to go, and since many knew about this hiding place (which had been in preparation for months), faced with imminent danger, they went in where they could. Thus, in a basement suitable for ten people, some 30 took shelter. Before climbing in, Yehezkel tore open pillows and scattered feathers everywhere to make it look as if the house had already been searched. Time began to pass. In terror they heard the same sounds over and over: shouts, shots, and dogs howling. Day and night all of them sat squeezed together, suffering from the heat. It was unbearable. Removing clothes, they were soon down to underwear. They did not eat and barely drank. An older man – nobody knew who he was or how he had gotten in – began to cough, causing great alarm. At one moment, they believed it was over because they heard a German in the house. As it was already night, he went away – Germans did not conduct searches during the hours of darkness.

The second night, with the water already gone, Yehezkel and some of the other young men went out in search of more. They approached the well but did not dare fill a container because making any noise was dangerous – the Germans were still there, waiting. Many bodies lay in the street. After entering several houses, they came across a half-full bucket, the hand of a dead woman submerged in it. They took it anyway. It was not enough for all, and people just wet their lips and went on waiting. All had agreed in advance not to abandon the shelter. In case of betrayal or discovery, they would toss a grenade and blow themselves up to keep from being sent to Sobibor.

The third night, several of the men climbed to the roof and realized there was no one to be seen anywhere in the city. No Germans, and the Poles had already looted all the houses. It was completely quiet. Returning to the cellar, they told the group it was time to escape to the woods, something few of them had dreamed of doing. Once out of the refuge, to their surprise they met up with 100 or so people on the street. The Lager's exit gate stood open. They ran and ran, hurrying past Falkenberg's house and at dawn arrived in a wooded area, stopping there. They did not know what to do – there was no plan, no leader, no food. Alexandra, Esther, Sara, her sisters, their mother, and Yehezkel (with his sister and brother) hid in this spot to rest.

Two days went by, when someone remarked there were still Jews at Adampol.[5] Several of the young men went to investigate and confirmed it was true. They decided to make the camp their destination – as it was known to be a place where Jews were taken in, allowed to work, and even if not paid, survived somehow.

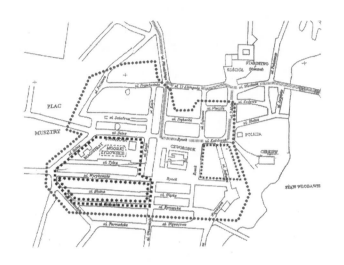

••••••••••• Area inhabited mostly by Jews until 1939.

ı ■ ■ ■ ■ ■ ■ ■ ■ ■ Jewish zone created in 1940.

▬▬▬▬▬ Place where Jews were assembled for roundups and displacement.

✱✱✱✱✱✱✱✱✱ Lager November 1942 - Abril 1943.

✶✶✶✶✶✶✶✶✶✶✶✶ Ghetto November 1942 - April 1943

Source: Dr. Krzysztof Skwirowski

10

THE SURVIVAL INSTINCT (HIL'S STORY)

On the morning of Thursday, May 21, 1942, Hil awoke to gunfire and shouting. The first Aktzia was about to begin. As he would observe years later, "That Thursday marked the beginning of the end for the Jews of Włodawa." With his work permit, he considered it safe to walk through the streets of the town, amid the reigning chaos. He had started working at the local sawmill, so he made his way there. After arriving, he left the premises with the manager to rescue any workers or members of their families who might have been detained. Only the old or infirm were supposed to appear at the market square for "relocation." The manager told Hil, "Do not worry. Dr. Ansel [the official in charge of deportations in Chelm] is a good friend of mine who owes me a lot of favors. If need be, I will get in touch with him."

When they got to the rynek they saw a large group of Jews heavily guarded by the SS, SA, and the Gendarmerie police. The Viennese Jews had come of their own volition since early on they had named their own executive committee which operated outside of the Judenrat, dealing directly with the Germans. Their representative had received the order and obeyed it to the letter. One of the Viennese arrivals had lodged in Grandmother Rosa's house. He was a senior prosecutor by the name of Friedjung, a second-generation

Christian with a Christian wife. The two were good friends with Falkenberg, who tried to save them from their destiny at Sobibor. He was unsuccessful though, because according to the racial laws Friedjung was Jewish by ancestry.

During this roundup, Falkenberg took an active interest in the fate of his employees. At 4 p.m. on Saturday, May 23, he appeared before those who were at work on the outskirts of town and told them not to return to the city until they received word from him: "The SS troops are unsatisfied. They are still hungry for victims. They may also take those with work permits." The workers waited until Falkenberg sent the message that they could return.[1] Meanwhile, the few people who had survived the massacre at the Zacheta theater, and those who had been detained on the streets, were all sent to Sobibor.

My father observed that during this first roundup, the Gestapo, in return for sizeable payments, gave refuge to several men and women who had hope that they would be spared. He laid the blame for this directly on Nitschke: "I wish to emphasize the fact that Nitschke gave the orders, while the others were simply onlookers. He had the power to pick out from the crowd skilled workers for special tasks, or those who paid him, or individuals he might choose for other reasons."

Amid the chaos that had been created, "About the only comfort we could offer one another was being able to talk about what we were suffering. Besides terror of the Germans – the mere sight of Nazis would cause panic – each of us was overcome by the fear of death by starvation." Yet life went on, and while there was much suffering, there were also cherished moments.

On Sunday, May 24, the second day of Shavuot, the Grunhaus family held a *Brit Milah* – the ritual of circumcision – for Moses, Hil's nephew, the son of his brother Leo. Jews did not forget their pact with God. They celebrated and toasted amidst their overwhelming sorrow. "Remarkable people, we Jews. We toasted with grieving hearts and eyes dried up from so many tears," were my father's words.

At last, some in town began to accept that the rumors about Sobibor were true, as Falkenberg would state much later: "In Włodawa people knew it. Sobibor was seven or eight kilometers away, and when you were working on the outskirts of town you could see the smoke from the camp's chimneys. It could rise at any time, and you would smell a disgusting sweetish odor ... They were killing Jews in gas ovens and burning the bodies."[2] The Germans strove to make their lies appear credible so as not to alarm the Jews, thus some doubted and kept up their hopes. In the area around Sobibor there were also forced labor camps. From each transport a few men were sent to one of them temporarily as a way of reinforcing the deception. Those selected were ordered to send postcards home saying everything was fine, and some of the messages reached Włodawa. Even with Sobibor being so close by with its smoke and smells, many discounted the evidence of extermination. They refused to accept it, for if they had, they would have lost hope and the strength to try to survive.

The conduct of the members of the Judenrat has been much debated. My father took an impartial view of the unrewarding and highly complicated task that fell to these men who were chosen to take charge of community matters amid so much violence and hardship. They had to mediate constantly between the excessive demands of the Germans and the urgent needs of their own people. As my father told us: "Many have criticized them, and they are still being criticized today. Far be it from me to do so. On the contrary, they deserve compassion and never criticism. With such a heavy burden on their shoulders, each of them tried to do his best. In such a situation ... there was no alternative; they were not angels. Each one tried to help ... under those conditions, in such difficult times, who could act any other way?"

Hil was constantly informed of what was going on. Maybe it was through Falkenberg that he heard about some of the isolated killings. The usual procedure was for the assassin to shoot the victim in the back of the neck while he or she was walking down the street. Then the body would be taken to the building housing the SS and the Judenrat, which would designate the gravediggers. Both groups knew in advance the identity of the condemned. Later, all the gravediggers were murdered.

July came, and toward the end of the month the Children's Roundup took place, an event that deeply affected Hil: "Impossible not to admire the strength of Rabbi Menahem Mendl Morgenstern who, dressed in his finest clothes, told the children stories, keeping them calm as they embarked on their last journey." He also quoted the words of another surviving witness: "I shall never forget the scene at the roundup of the children: their heroism and pride, the courage and stance of the rabbi, his contemptuous looks directed at the guards. That horrific image haunts me and will haunt me forever."[3] After the war, when Nitschke attempted to deny having personally overseen the Aktzia, several survivors – my father among them – pointed out his direct responsibility.

On October 23, 1942, people began to suspect that something was about to happen. Whenever a roundup was in the works, the Germans would reinforce the Ukrainian and Lithuanian security contingents and bring several empty freight cars to the train station. And so the fateful day came. Saturday, October 24, marked the beginning of the Great Roundup – the Black Shabbat. Eight days previously, Nitschke had ordered all Jews in the surrounding area to congregate in the city. On Thursday night, 22 October, they were all brought into town during a heavy downpour and had to remain on the streets because there was nowhere to lodge them. The next day, supervisors received orders not to go out to their worksites on Saturday, and the word was spread around the city.

Hil and his brother Leo did not notice anything unusual on Friday night when they went to bed, and they slept peacefully until heavy artillery fire awakened them. It was still dark. Once outside, they saw people running and immediately realized what was happening. The brothers got their mother and Leo's wife and children and headed to Falkenberg's house. Since all of them were known to the Germans, there seemed no reason to hide. They believed their work permits would protect them.

Because Włodawa was flooded with people, the Germans did not do organized house-to-house searches during this roundup. They did raid homes on the main street, however. Reaching Falkenberg's residence, they fired into the air and shouted, "Jews out!" but dared not enter. Falkenberg, not afraid to face the Germans, berated them for the attempt to penetrate what was "German territory." Then Nitschke appeared with his huge dog. Falkenberg talked to him, trying to save the workers. Nitschke insisted that he hand over the Jews he was harboring. In the end 30 were taken, the rest staying hidden in the bedroom of Falkenberg's wife, in the cellar, and in the granary. Once the 30 were outside, menacing shouts could be heard: "Hands up! Get moving!" Hil and Leo, among the arrested, consoled themselves with the knowledge that their family was still in Falkenberg's house and would be spared. As the 30 began walking, more and more detainees joined the group, including women and children escorted by other SS officers. Finally, all arrived at the sports field where the entire Judenrat stood, heavily guarded. Nitschke soon appeared, accompanied by officials from the Lublin Gestapo. He looked over the scene at length, then left. Fifteen minutes later he was back with his aides and began to pull people out of the ranks: the head of the Judenrat, one of its members, shoemakers, tailors, and other artisans who worked for the Germans, plus Hil and Leo. These 50 to 70 individuals were then shut up in the courtyard of the nearby Gestapo office. Hil, Leo, and the rest could only imagine what was happening to those still on the sports field – now including Hil's mother, his fiancée, and Leo's wife and children who had been arrested along with others found in Falkenberg's house. Some desperately tried to join their families, but they were stopped by the guards. There was nothing they could do.

In this roundup the Germans captured several thousand Jews, many violently dragged out of their hiding places. Nitschke supervised his own people as well as the members of the Gendarmerie, the Ukrainians, and the Lithuanians. All of them totally merciless – hitting, stabbing, or even riddling with bullets anybody who showed a hint of resistance. And indeed, many witnesses pointed to Nitschke as the perpetrator of several murders. The troops led the prisoners to the train station on foot; those unable to walk were shot. Many young people headed for the station voluntarily, hoping they would be saved by their work permits, reasoning the Germans would only choose those unable to work – the sick, the disabled, the elderly. Those left locked inside the Gestapo's courtyard, powerless, were prey to despair. Years later, my father wrote: "The 70 of us could see nothing, our eyes blinded, our hearts hardened, each of us feeling guilty and wretched for being a survivor. Ready to walk with everybody else, we lacked the courage to do so. The question of why exactly we had been spared was eating us up. We realized we had to save ourselves at any cost." Meanwhile, Falkenberg, Lemanschik, and Antoniewicz arrived and spoke to them through the barbed wire. The detainees begged them to save any that they could. Then, when Nitschke appeared with his dog, they appealed to him, and he assured them falsely that he would be bringing back those who had work permits.

After the war, Falkenberg described the roundup in detail. "This act was beyond abominable. Nitschke was there with his enormous dog and anybody who disobeyed was savagely beaten. Nitschke did not listen and said I had better take off; if I did not, I too might be apprehended. The Jews were struck with clubs and set upon by dogs ... Once the detainees were all gathered, the Germans moved them in trains used to transport animals. People had to stand up, one behind the other. The elderly Jews who could not walk any longer and wanted to get out of the line were ill-treated by the sentinels, who hit them with the butts of their rifles, even punching one of them in the back and throwing him off the train. Nitschke directed the entire operation."[4]

In her testimony, survivor Tamara Turkienicz gave a detailed description of the chaos that prevailed: "As we walked, they kept hitting us hard. Shots rang out, and many Jews fell under the bullets. We ran into corpses on the road and had to step over them ... there was no stopping, or we would be killed. The Germans did not allow moving of the wounded. Along the Bug River, many young people,

85

trying to save themselves at any cost, jumped into the water. The Nazi bullets reached them there. We arrived at the station where the train was waiting. The guards hit us and shouted at us."

Franz Holtzheimer corroborated these accounts. He and Falkenberg were allowed to pull 400 workers out of the line, rescuing them. To accomplish this, he had maneuvered through the crowd, moving among thousands of Jews, thus witnessing firsthand the atrocities of the roundup. Holtzheimer also stated that as he traveled from Chelm to Włodawa on the first morning of that Aktzia, he had seen many corpses by the side of the road – the bodies of Jews caught in the surrounding area and forced to head for Włodawa. My father described the emotions of those taken out of the death lines: "After the others departed, the Germans sent us home ... embittered, saddened, empty." His mother did not return but Ida, his fiancée, did. Leo's family came back too, having managed somehow to survive.

Once the roundup was over, many Jews emerged from various hiding places, one of which was Falkenberg's granary. Years later, Falkenberg explained how he concealed people there. When he contracted typhus, a Jewish physician named Springer had treated him, and Falkenberg took the opportunity to discuss with the doctor the feasibility of allowing a few people to stay inside the hayloft without suffocating. Following Springer's advice, he built a square structure using bales of hay stored on a piece of land that adjoined his property, leaving some openings in the center to allow air to circulate. During the third Aktzia many rushed to this place up in the loft, closing the bales around them from the inside with hooks. When the SD and the Gendarmerie arrived with their dogs, they exclaimed, "We had better set fire to the granary, surely there must be Jews inside." To which Falkenberg replied, "I bet my bottom dollar there is nobody in there. And, even if there were two or three Jews inside, is it worth it to leave the horses without food?"[5] The dogs sniffed the area, but they did not pick up a scent or find a way in. All the Jews who hid in the loft survived.

The number of victims in this extermination operation varies according to sources. It is estimated as somewhere between 5,400 and 6,000. In the same roundup the Germans sent 2,000 people to Sobibor who had walked from Chelm to Włodawa. All of them were gassed upon arrival at the concentration camp.

The day after it was all over, besides those from Falkenberg's granary, many of the Jews who had escaped at dawn returned to the city. There were more than 2,000 Jews left in Włodawa. It was then that the Germans marked off a territory that went from one side of the Lager to the other side of the ghetto, an action that gave rise to an indescribable struggle to be in the Lager. Hil and Leo returned to their work at the sawmill, relieved to go on living, yet with heavy hearts because of losing so much family.

By that time, Hil had obtained false papers with the Aryan name of Henryk Gajda. In one of his testimonial statements, he said that Falkenberg had provided him with the documents. The first of two, dated October 12, 1942, was an identity card, or *Kennkarte*, issued in Warsaw, stating the city as his workplace. It was renewed in Bauerwitz (now Baborów, Poland) on October 12, 1944. The second, dated October 23, 1942, was issued in Wyryki on that date, and included the name of his supposed parents. Both documents specified his religion as Catholic.

Several days went by and on November 7 the fourth Aktzia took place, this time only affecting the ghetto. Many Jewish policemen were caught, as well as the members of the Judenrat who were still alive. The operation lasted around three days and some survived because they had places to hide around the clock. Among those not discovered were Leo and his family, Grandfather Moses and his wife and children, and Joseph and his family. Once again Falkenberg concealed many people in his hayloft. By this time all his workers had numbers to wear on their chests but many Jews who had taken refuge in the Lager did not. Falkenberg was aware of that and let such individuals stay in his granary anyway.

87

After this roundup the Nazis appointed a new Judenrat. In the words of my father, a relatively calm period began. And there was tranquility in the ghetto: "People wanted to think that maybe ... they tried not to think, they did not want to see, they did not want to believe ...." Hil and Leo were living in the Lager and went on working at the sawmill. "Things progressed smoothly. The administrators were asked to provide the manpower and they kept assuring us there would be no more roundups and, listening to the news from the battlefield, we assumed that would indeed be the case."

Hundreds of Jews kept arriving from villages, neighboring towns, and the woods. They imagined that the German decision to make the city a *Judenstadt* would turn it into a safe place – the last deception for the Jews of Włodawa. The Nazis kept the truth of their final destiny a deep secret. At first, they assured Jews they would be relocated or sent to work camps; later they promoted the illusion that those with work permits would not be detained. The Jews believed them, for it was necessary to cling to some hope if one was to go on living. By the time it became clear that the objective was total extermination it was almost impossible to find avenues of escape. The only remaining way out was to join the area's partisans, who appeared from time to time in the Lager and the ghetto. Most people opted for readying their hiding places, realizing it was only a temporary solution. As my father said, that was how they kept their hopes up.

"We celebrated Hanukkah and Purim. Passover was approaching, and we made *matzos*. The holiday was joyful, since we could see the Germans would be losing the war, and our hopes rose more and more. It was simply a matter of obeying the work supervisors and living in peace with the Gendarmerie," my father observed later. Time went along until April 30, 1943. On the morning of May 1, Włodawa awoke to gunfire. The previous day, in the greatest secrecy, the askaris had come back to Włodawa under the command of the Chelm Gestapo. Nitschke returned with his crew but this time they were not in charge of the roundup. Heavily armed men surrounded the work camp and the ghetto. Once again, the shouts were heard, "Jews, come out!" The fifth Aktzia was underway.[6]

This time they did house-to-house searches. Everyone caught was led to the market square and then ordered to keep walking. Hil was in hiding with a group of 30 other people, including Leo and his wife and children. One of the little ones coughed, giving them away. They were surrounded, Hil escaped at a run – dodging bullets and taking shelter in an attic on Wyrykowska Street. The wife of a Viennese doctor climbed up behind him. "Since it was already dark, the Germans were fearful and stopped searching." He stayed there until the next day and through the gaps in the wall observed people being taken away: carts came to load up those who had been snatched from their homes.

Night fell once more. "I wanted to leave my hideout, taking my Aryan identity card and get away. The doctor's wife begged me not to. She was right because the work camp and the ghetto were closely watched. They resumed house-to-house searches and found us, ordering us to remove our clothes, which they searched. We got dressed and went down to the street. Outside were more Gestapo officers. Mrs. Falkenberg arrived – her husband had taken ill – and she convinced the Gestapo to leave some workers," my father recalled.

The Gestapo agents changed their minds and went from house to house shouting for the Jews to come out, that they would be letting them work under Falkenberg. Then Mrs. Falkenberg chose Hil and the doctor's wife to join the group, along with 50 women and 30 men, whom she lodged in the granary at her house. A sizeable number of Jews had fled to the woods, others had ended up taking refuge at Adampol where there was work. Hil's fiancée Ida, and Leo and his family all perished in this fifth and final roundup. Such great sadness for my father in realizing he was not able to save them. He had always known how to choose the right path but in this instance, he had run out of choices and luck.

Falkenberg appeared Sunday and was able to warn Hil to get away immediately. He barely had time to flee before the Germans arrived and took all the men but five and murdered them. Hil ran to his mother's house and hid in the woodpile until dark. Then he returned to Falkenberg's until Wednesday when some partisans from Moshe Lichtenberg's group arrived. Hil took off with them.

The 50 women left were given the job of cleaning the Jews' abandoned houses. Later most of them were murdered. Those able to escape did so with help from Falkenberg. One night, he got all the Ukrainian guards so drunk they passed out. Then the women, following Falkenberg's advice, fled to Adampol. In farewell, he said to them, "Any one of you who survives, please, look me up and let me know you are alive."[7] Falkenberg himself provided another version, confirming that in June there were still close to 100 Jews on his property. Officials at the Chelm station decided it was time to exterminate them and phoned Falkenberg to inform him. He repeated loud and clear what they were saying at the other end of the line so the Jews would hear and escape. When the Germans arrived the next morning and asked him where the Jews were, Falkenberg said he had no idea. The Germans left.

In 1943, Hil Grunhaus was 39 years old. Joining Lichtenberg's group, he found himself obliged to match the pace of these young people as they moved around from place to place. Doing so much walking, he hurt his foot and could not keep up with them. He asked Lichtenberg to help him find a secure hideout and offered him part of the money he had stashed away in the Włodawa house. The partisans went to Włodawa by night to fetch the money. Then they were able to get a Polish farmer named Szerpiński to lodge Hil in exchange for a substantial payment. The man's farm was in the village of Podpakule, about 22 kilometers from Włodawa. Hil also bought a machine gun from Szerpiński, which he donated to the partisans. He was crafty and managed to keep a small fortune on his person, gold pieces hidden in a money belt that he wore. He stayed at the farm a few months, relatively safe there, with the partisans visiting periodically to see that all was well.

In July, when he was beginning to anticipate that it was time to move on, Alexandra arrived at the same farm. That made his departure more urgent. "With two of us here it becomes especially dangerous. I am going to Warsaw," he told her. Afraid to be recognized by the Germans if he traveled by train, he offered to pay the farmer to transport him in his wagon, using a travel permit allowing him to go from Włodawa to Warsaw by way of Chelm and Lublin. It was issued in Włodawa on July 16 and was in effect from July 17 to August 17. And so Hil departed for Warsaw, leaving Alexandra at the farm. The trip of 400 kilometers lasted several days, fortunately without a mishap.

Once in Warsaw, he rented a room, having decided that the city was a good place to hide. He knew it well and a friend had promised him a safe haven: "Come, you will not have any problem." Also, another friend lived there, a dentist named Zielinski, with whom he had left some gold pieces. With good false documents and a perfect command of Polish, the fair-haired, green-eyed Hil could move around Warsaw without great concern.

11

THE ROAD TAKEN

Reaching Adampol, Alexandra and Esther and their group met up
with other Jews who had escaped from Włodawa. The new arrivals
made themselves as comfortable as possible but went to sleep hungry
and thirsty. They hoped they might be able to work for Willy Selinger
in exchange for food since he ran a rather open camp. Several
partisan groups passed through Adampol regularly, making it a
relatively easy place from which to escape. But the camp by this time,
mid-May 1943, was overcrowded and could not accommodate them,
so they had to look elsewhere. They chose a nearby village called
Natalin, moving into an abandoned house. They could work there in
a brick factory, also under Selinger's control, and in the gardens of
local farmers. The pay was little. Esther had managed to bring along
two rolls of fabric from her father's store and selling some pieces to
buy food helped them survive. One night someone stole the cloth
that was left. They began to go hungry, making it urgent to get in
touch with the partisans.

Meanwhile, the sisters were anxiously wondering what might have
happened to their father and the rest of the family. Esther, once again
showing how truly brave she was, decided to go back to Włodawa
with one of Sara's sisters to try to get news. It was night and no one

was found in the Lager. The 50 women the Germans had kept alive to clean and clear out Jewish houses were in Falkenberg's granary. While attempting to go to the place where Esther's father had hidden, the two girls heard shooting and, frightened, went back to Natalin. Trying again the next night, Esther made it there, but the hiding place was empty. She ran into a cousin who told her that six or seven days after the roundup, the cleaning women were searching in the Jewish houses, accompanied by a German. As they walked into the building where Moses and his family were hiding, the cleaners were speaking Yiddish to one another. Hearing those voices, Moses revealed himself and encountered a German. The whole family was taken out by force. The cousin said that the terrified children refused to move, the Germans dragging them out violently, thoughtlessly. The cleaners did not want to say what happened to the family.

Alexandra and Esther found themselves dealing with the almost certain loss of the last of their family. Murdered where they were found or sent to Sobibor, by then all of them were most likely dead. It must have been a harsh blow for the two girls but the desire to go on living gave them the strength necessary to keep moving forward. My mother told us that after the war ended, she kept hoping to find one of her loved ones alive.

The group's situation improved for a short time with the arrival of Srulik Feferman, a religious youngster of 13 who came with his 11-year-old brother. Sara knew the children, who had lost their entire family. Before he was killed, Srulik's father told the boy where he had put his money. Sara advised him to go retrieve it and he did so. When he returned, they were all stunned – there was so much, bills and gold coins. "A treasure trove!" as Sara put it. Both youngsters stayed with the girls, who sewed the money into Srulik's clothes. Periodically they took a little to buy food for all, so at least for a moment they did not go hungry.

Members of various partisan groups arrived in the area to visit their families. The ones the girls knew best were those in Moshe Lichtenberg's group, as almost all of them were from Włodawa.

Several times, Sara, Esther, and Alexandra scoured nearby villages, chatting with Jews in an effort to locate them, to contact them. The girls were not completely free to move around. They could explore cautiously along trails on the edge of the woods and – if they sensed some danger – run and hide quickly among the trees. They were desperate and fearful; besides the Germans, the area was infested with criminals. Once when Sara and Esther were out, two men grabbed them from behind, giving them a terrible scare. Esther reacted shrewdly, taking off her watch and handing it to the man; Sara, who could see Esther from the corner of her eye, quickly followed suit and they escaped.

One day, aware that a roundup had begun at Adampol, the girls hurried to a nearby wooded area. It was early summer and Esther, with her instinct for making good decisions, saw a field of tall wheat on the other side of the trees that looked like a good place to hide. Luck was with them, and despite the German's passing so near their voices could be heard, the girls lay there, not moving, until the roundup was over. Sara and her sisters did the same but those who ran to conceal themselves in the woods perished. Srulik and his brother did not appear. They finally found them, with Srulik dead and his grief-stricken little brother sitting beside him. Unstitching the coins and bills from Srulik's clothes, the girls gave the money to the brother and advised him to seek out a group of religious Jews hidden in the woods and take refuge with them. They knew no more of him.

Alexandra and Sara would go out regularly to look for the partisans until one day they finally encountered their friend Srulke Fishman outside of Adampol. Talking with him, Alexandra was told that her cousin Yankele Lederman had been looking for her to give her 500 złotys so she could eat. Srulke belonged to Moshe Lichtenberg's group. Sara recalled that he took them to the camp where they spoke with Moshe. Hearing Alexandra's name, he asked whether she was related to Hil Grunhaus, and when she said she was, he explained they had just found Hil a hideout with a farmer in Podpakule. One of the partisans said, "You ought to join Hil" and promised to ask the

Polish farmer if he would agree to keep Esther and Alexandra on his farm also.

The partisans were aware Jews should not stay in places where they could be easily seen. "You have to save yourselves; you have to protect yourselves because the Germans will come here, and they will kill you." Up to then the Lichtenberg group had not accepted women but that was about to change. Meanwhile Alexandra wrote a letter she gave the partisans to deliver to Hil. They returned and told the sisters that only one of them could go to the farm. Since Esther was older it was she who decided, saying to her sister, "You go. I'll manage." Once again Esther's resolve sealed the fate of the two. At the cost of her own life, she saved Alexandra's. Not long after, sometime in July 1943, two partisans came to get Alexandra. Esther accompanied her as far as she could. Neither of them imagined – even if they might well have suspected it – that this would be their final farewell, but it was the last time they ever saw each other.

Alexandra spent about a week with the partisans, sharing their way of life as they took her to the farm. During the journey, for the first time in four years, she had a sense of freedom. The night before arriving at her refuge, she wrote Sara a seven-page letter – by candlelight no doubt –in pencil on scraps of paper. By this time Sara was almost certainly with Moshe Lichtenberg's partisans, and the two groups transmitted messages back and forth. The letter is a moving testimonial that reveals her sadness and, above all, her overwhelming anguish at that time of uncertainty.

Dear Sara,

We have arrived. I went through so much on the road that I cannot describe. Certainly, the guys will tell you about it. If I wanted to do so, I would not have enough paper. Everything turned out as planned and I was with them the whole time. I shall never forget these days. Imagine, Surca, me in all those places, at night, on the road, singing and whistling ... It was something extraordinary. On sunny days we sang, and we walked with caution. I was very safe with those guys and completely free to have someone to talk to. I cannot write all that happened to us on the journey. Besides, there are things that cannot be written about.

It is three in the morning. The hour is approaching when I will have to leave the group. My heart is beating fast. In all this time I have avoided thinking about this moment. In a few hours I will be alone and begin my life in the wilderness. Who knows when I will be able to have news of all of you? Such words would be a great comfort to me. Surca, I have to stop writing because the tears are flowing. Can you imagine how painful it is for me to write this letter?

I do not have much to write about myself, except that tonight they are taking me to a safe place. I know I will not be lacking anything, and I wonder what my life will become. They all say things will go well; nobody can understand [my anguish]. Only you know what I am thinking. There is so much to tell but I can only do that when we are face to face.

I have to stop writing. I cannot control my weeping. I am sure we are not going to meet again before we die.

I cannot write home. Write for me since I could not bear to. Write Esther, tell her from me that she should think hard about how to save herself. Tell her to write me in detail about what she is doing and what is happening with her. Ask them to write me individually so I will have more to read.

My skirt got torn on the road. I did not notice how it happened. Ask Esther to send me clothes.

Surca, answer as soon as you get this letter. Write and tell me everything that has happened to you. I am interested in every detail. In my next letter I will tell you more. During the journey I thought about you the whole time, without forgetting you for a moment. It would make me so happy if I could see you again. Day and night I would tell you all that has happened to me, and we would not stop talking. Now I will not write more for fear that someone might find the letters.

The guys treated me very well. You could go to the ends of the earth with them.

I am ending this letter. I do not know when I can write again. Surca, it makes my heart so heavy but still I must take responsibility for my own life. Perhaps that is the fate I deserve. When you have read this letter, destroy it, so no one else can read it. I do not want people pitying me. When we were in the woods, I encouraged the girls, telling them they ought to rise above adversity. I told them not to feel sorry for me since I was not as badly off as they imagined. You are the only one to whom I can speak the truth to.

I am going to keep your letters and those from home because this is all I will have left.

Goodbye for now.

We also have a letter written by Esther in late July.

Dear Sister,

What is happening that I have not received a letter? I do not understand. Have you not had a chance to send me a few words? I know nothing about what is happening to you. How do you live? How are you doing? How do you spend the days? Are you at peace? I believe I have a right to hear what is going on with you. I only know you are in that place, nothing else. Surca wrote to me. Dear one, you know how much it means to me to get a letter from you. Please take any opportunity to write me.

How is Hil? Is he doing well? Write me in detail what is happening with you. I, for example, write you every day, for me it is like talking to you. In that way I think you are with me. It is my only pleasure. May God keep you.

Sheindele, have you seen father and our sisters and brothers in your dreams? Once I dreamed about father and Joseph. They were quite far away, and they looked sad. They did not see me.

Sheindele, where we are it is not peaceful. I did not think I would still be here today. The inspector told us there is going to be an Aktzia. People are running away. Everything is falling apart. But we stay in the same place ourselves with no hope ... [illegible] cannot move and besides all the roads are closed. So, we wait without moving. What will happen tomorrow? Thus, we live day to day. News came to me that the decision to stay was the best one. Aunt Leah and Zlatko were murdered and also many others.

I end this letter. I send you a big kiss. God be willing and may our paths soon cross, just as they did up to now.

Esther

With great sadness Sara left her mother, her sisters, and Esther at Adampol when she joined Moshe Lichtenberg's partisans who by then were accepting women. She made Lichtenberg promise they would go back to fetch the other women. But before he could do so several of them came down with typhus, among them Esther, which left them unable to leave.

It is not clear how long Esther survived at Adampol. It was probably until one of the two final roundups, occurring between August 6–8 and August 13–15, 1943. During those days, the Germans killed 680 Jews at the camp and buried them in a mass grave. Sometime later, in the spring of 1944, a civilian group under the command of German forces dug up the grave and burned all the corpses.

While Sara was with the partisans, she received several letters from her sisters. In one of them, they remarked that Esther was ill, begging her to please not mention it to Alexandra who found out at the end of the war when she met up with Sara again in Włodawa.

At the end of July 1943, when Alexandra arrived at the farm, she met Hil there. He had to leave for Warsaw and explained that he would send for her later. Hil and Alexandra were second cousins and knew each other's families well. Probably due to their age difference they did not have any contact before then.

Alexandra remained at the farm about four months. She slept in the attic because the farmer was afraid the Germans would find out a Jew was there – he too was in danger of being killed. The farmer had a relationship with the partisans and had sold them arms but he also had a reputation as a bandit who had killed a Jew. However, he did not denounce her or Hil, fearing the partisans more than the Germans. The partisans considered a Jew would be safe with him. The farmer and his family treated Alexandra well. During all those months she did not go hungry. There was a daughter, a nice young woman, who would bring her wool or thread to knit the family sweaters and other items. Sometimes she slept at the daughter's house, spending a month there, and then going to the home of a sister of the farmer for another month, then rotating again. Her days were spent in the attic, not going outside and only using the bathroom at night. There was little conversation with those on the farm although the roundup at Adampol was mentioned by the farmer who had heard about it in Włodawa. The news made her immensely sad and lonely, while at the same time she held on to the hope that Esther might have survived.

In November, Hil asked his good friend Zielinski, a Polish dentist from Włodawa, to go get her. Zielinski's Jewish wife had been murdered by the Germans and he agreed to escort Alexandra to Warsaw. He brought her money, an old coat, and a fake document. She was frightened about taking the train, so they asked a Polish partisan who was a friend of the farmer's daughter whether he thought they could get away with it. The partisan encouraged them to go since right at that time many people were on the move and the commotion would help them pass unnoticed. They decided to try.

Arriving at the Chelm station, they found that the Warsaw train had already departed. They had to wait until morning for the next train. It was extremely cold and the wait was terrible. The station was full of drunk Germans who shouted and carried on all night. The dentist sat far from her since it would have been quite dangerous for them to be seen together. Alexandra, trembling with fright, tied a scarf around her face as if suffering from toothache. She wrapped herself in the coat and lay down on a bench, trying to make herself quiet and invisible. It was on this endless night that she recalled feeling the closest to danger.

The next morning, they took the train. The Pole warned her, "If they catch you, do not give me away." They boarded the train separately and sat far from each other. When the conductor came to check the tickets, he realized right away that Alexandra was Jewish because she was poorly dressed and pale after all those months in the attic. He approached, asking for her ticket, saying, "Rare ... rare ... rare bird, you do not see many of these anymore." But he did not report her. Seeing how young she was – only 19 – he took pity on her. Surely, that conductor was a good person. She was lucky, very lucky.

At last, they arrived in Warsaw. They got into a wagon and the Pole took her to the apartment of a single woman on Marszalkowska Street, the city's main avenue. Hil had made the necessary arrangements for her lodging. Once more, her fate had been decided by another person – this time it was Hil Grunhaus.

12

CRUCIAL DECISIONS

Years later, my mother described how she quickly adapted to her new lodgings in Warsaw: "I recall the surname Bondarska, I have forgotten her first name. A single woman of about 50 years old, living alone who never had visitors. I got along fine there. In need, she took me in because Hil was paying her, which meant being able to eat. Very much afraid, the lady would go out in the morning, return for lunch, then take off again until dark. Zielinski, the dentist, would also appear at noon and the three of us ate together." My mother talked about Mrs. Bondarska warmly and used to say that it would have been nice to see her again after the war.

Alexandra spent nine months there, indoors, in that same apartment all the time, until August 1944. Never having been in Warsaw, it would have been hard for her to get about on her own. To make the confinement bearable, she devoted herself to reading. Mrs. Bondarska brought her books from the library – Tolstoy, Dostoevsky, Thomas Mann. Alexandra was afraid to leave the house. Even though she had a good identity card which had belonged to a deceased daughter of the farmer in Podpakule, this did not reassure her. With a photo of herself she had a new card fabricated with the same false name adopted in November 1942: Alexandra Charkiewitsch. She spoke good Polish but was aware that Poles easily recognized Jews. Any detail, no matter how insignificant, could give someone away: accent, mannerisms, gestures, gait, even an expression that might show fear. The city was rife with *szmalcowniks* – blackmailers dedicated to recognizing Jews – along with the German police and the so-called blue police of the Poles. The danger on the streets was great, another reason not to venture far from her refuge.

Marszalkowska Street is, as it was then, a main thoroughfare in Warsaw. Alexandra was probably able to make out much of the city from there. Did she peer out the window? Or was that also too risky? Perhaps by night she looked at the streetlights and the buildings. What ideas went through her mind? The food was adequate, and I never heard her say she could not move around the apartment. I believe that being inside those walls comforted her; although knowing it was not possible to hide there forever must have caused her to worry about the future.

Hil was also in Warsaw, with other people in a different household, since it was not wise for them to stay together; if something were to happen to one of them, the other would have a chance to get away. Only on rare occasions did he visit Alexandra. Since his friend Zielinski saw her every day, he would have kept Hil informed of her welfare. Hil went by the name of Henryk Gajda: he kept the identity document issued back in 1942 in Wyryki, near Włodawa, since it had been forged quite well. We know little of his doings during that period. He lacked nothing, as he had gold coins cleverly hidden in his money belt, and Zielinski was guarding the rest of his money and valuables. I remember my mother speaking of my father's money belt with humor. He always seemed to find a way to provide for himself. Thanks to his deep interest in politics, Hil was also up to date on the latest happenings. When visiting Alexandra, he would report to her what was going on.

The year 1944 marked a definite change in the war. By now it was obvious that Germany was going to lose. Halfway through the year, eastern Poland was liberated: Włodawa and Chelm on July 21, and

Lublin on July 24. If Hil and Alexandra had been able to remain in the Włodawa area, they would have been free sooner. In Warsaw, news that the Russians were on their way kept the population anxious and hopeful – but events proved otherwise.

The *AK* (the National Army or Armia Krajowa) – the main movement of Polish resistance during the Second World War – was planning a general uprising to take place when the Germans began to pull out. On the one hand, the Poles were compelled to protect the civilian population (which was already stockpiling food and water), on the other hand, they needed to aid the Soviet advance, all the while trying to facilitate the possible creation of a Polish army. In the final days of July, the Russians reached the other side of the Vistula River on the outskirts of Warsaw and stopped there. The Germans then began to regroup their forces, which meant it was time for the uprising to begin – and it did, on August 1, 1944. The first days saw an atmosphere of great euphoria. There was a spirit of victory. In the areas that fell into Polish hands, the population helped as best they could. The joy was short-lived, however – five days later the Germans began taking back control and regaining their foothold.

Hil went to join Alexandra. Early on, the Poles laid claim to half the city but the two were still in the German part. Little by little, the Germans recaptured various areas, evacuating the Polish population. They started bombing and fighting, going from house to house, razing all the buildings. Himmler had ordered the destruction of Warsaw. As my mother told us later, when the Germans arrived, she and Hil were ordered out of the building. They obeyed and fortunately their documents were not inspected. Once in the street, the Germans shouted, "Go to the right!" then kept shooting. They ran two blocks, somehow avoiding the bullets, and at last entered the Polish zone.

That is when they became Polish refugees. Only Mrs. Bondarska, who had escaped on her own, knew they were Jewish. The Poles showed great solidarity during the rebellion and did not question anyone's identity. The two of them felt little danger of being recognized as Jews, passing as Poles quite easily. Having abandoned the building in a hurry, they had fled without food and had no idea of where to find it. Luckily, they came to a refugee area where soup was provided once a day from the Polish army. My mother recalled living there for six terrible weeks, hungry and fearing both the Poles and the Germans. They had never suffered such deprivation, reaching the point of seeking bits of food by scraping out abandoned cooking pots.

In September, the situation worsened. Food and water were scarce, there was no electricity, and the sanitary conditions were deplorable – which increased the risk of illness. Occasionally the Allies and the Russians dropped supplies by air. The support of the civilian population was fading away because the rebellion had been unsuccessful. In some zones controlled by the AK where adequate supplies of water, food, and medicine were available, conditions were better. The advancing Germans had been gradually reclaiming territory, with Hil and Alexandra finding themselves once again in an enemy zone. Many wanted to surrender. When the Allies saw the Russians at the gates of Warsaw they held back, hoping that the Soviets would go in; however, that did not happen. Politically, it was in the interest of the Russians not to intervene and to let the Poles liberate Warsaw – then Russia would take over, install their communist regime, and keep the Polish government (in exile in London) from returning. But at the end of September the Poles surrendered, and on October 1, the Germans ordered the total evacuation of Warsaw.

The population left in short order. It is estimated that between 166,000 and 200,000 people died, more than 500,000 were evacuated, and 50 percent of the city was destroyed completely. Supposedly by that time there were no Jews left in Warsaw. Of those who had been in hiding, 17,000 died during the rebellion.

Before the general evacuation in October 1944, two other voluntary exoduses had taken place. Those in the city faced the dilemma of whether to stay hidden and await the arrival of the Soviets (who were already on the outskirts of town) or to leave as they had been ordered to do. Hil feared that a city in ruins and full of Germans was too great a risk, deciding it was better to leave. He and Alexandra joined the general departure of the civilian population. If they had stayed, they would have had to wait many weeks for liberation – until January 17, 1945, the day the Soviets entered Warsaw. My mother used to say my father made wise decisions, and besides that, he was almost always lucky: "One had to have luck in making the right decisions."

To expedite the evacuation, the Germans separated the old from the young. Under dreadful conditions most of the population was sent to various nearby work camps. The biggest one, Pruszków, took in the greatest number and the rest were sent elsewhere. Hil and Alexandra went to one of the smaller ones, name unknown. Conditions were bad in these places and once there, people were assigned to forced labor in Germany or sent to concentration camps or to the interior of Poland, an area still under German control. Once again, the two had to make some crucial decisions about their future, and once again, Hil took a chance: they volunteered to work in Germany. To Hil, the further away from the Poles they could get the safer they would be, even in the enemy's country.

They never described those awful days they spent crowded together with the Poles, who might have recognized them, or their fear at that point of what the future might hold. The trip to Germany was equally tortuous: for three days they traveled in closed cattle cars – with no food, water, or toilets – overcome with terror, thinking they would end up like all the Jews sent to extermination camps. On October 15, the train discharged its passengers at the Bauerwitz Station in Upper Silesia, where some older Germans were looking for workers since the young men of the region were serving in the army. Right away Hil got a job in a potato flour mill. Things were more difficult for Alexandra. She was so young and looked pale and fragile after almost a year spent indoors. Along with them there were 3,000 Poles in the same situation. The two were quite frightened: to be among so many Poles was extremely dangerous. Hil advised Alexandra to get any kind of work immediately. When some farmers arrived seeking help, she volunteered but nobody chose her: they picked all the rest, and she was the last one left. Finally, a man in his 70s approached her with his wife: "Well, I am going to hire you although you are quite skinny. I do not think you are going to be able to work." The couple had a farm with animals on the outskirts of Leobschütz (today, Glubczyce), quite far from where Hil was going to be working.

Alexandra soon began her stay on the farm, a completely new environment for someone who had never been to Germany. Several members of the old couple's family were there also: a hunchback son, a daughter whose husband had been drafted, and a four-year-old granddaughter. There was also a Ukrainian worker. Since autumn had just arrived, there was a lot of work, and the days were long. They would rise at four in the morning to go to the fields and return at nine in the evening. Alexandra had to adapt to the routine and by night was exhausted. The first task was harvesting the wheat, newly ripe. Fortunately, when winter began the harvest was over and there was less to do. The farm had pigs, horses, and four or five milk cows. One day, the farmer's wife asked Alexandra to do the milking, a skill completely foreign to this city girl. The alternative offered was cleaning the stable. *No way can I do that*, she thought. So she said to the woman, "If you teach me how to milk a cow, I will learn," and she did. Every morning and every night, she milked all the cows except for one, a kicker, who was left to the farmer's wife or the Ukrainian who cleaned the stable. Never having studied any German, little by little she began practicing. The couple knew nothing about the war or what was happening to the Jews. The farmer's wife told her she used to have some Jewish friends, but they must have all emigrated to Palestine.

In the town were many foreign workers who attended Sunday mass. Since she was supposedly a Polish Catholic and did not want to call attention to herself, Alexandra decided to go with them. During mass she did not know how to act, but she managed to imitate the farmer's daughter. As time went on she gained self-confidence, overcame some of her fear, and began to join in more with the Poles. Once a friend told her a Pole had spread a rumor that she was Jewish. Terrified, she contacted Hil who quickly came to her aid. He threatened the Pole, and the matter was forgotten. There was a Czech who took to her and when he was about to flee, he asked her to go with him. Always a pretty girl, being in the country had restored the glow of her complexion. Except for the week with the partisans en route to Podpakule, for the first time in five years she was enjoying the freedom to move around, often going to the village to run errands for the farmer's wife. Those were special moments when she delighted in walking along through the trees, with the sun and the winter cold stinging her cheeks. The country smells, the landscape, were a source of pleasure.

It is generally assumed that the Poles who evacuated Warsaw and were sent to Germany were subjected to "forced labor," but Hil and Alexandra's experience was not like that. Of course, they were not allowed to move to other places and were in fact afraid to try, for that would have been quite risky. In Leobschütz the tasks were simple, and the farm people were kind to Alexandra, treating her well and making her feel like a human being again. The papers she had obtained in Warsaw enabled her to apply for an official document: an employment permit that provided security. Issued on November 30, 1944, in Gaszowice, Leobschütz County, the card authorized her to work on the farm of Eduard Kosch and declared she could not leave his employment or move elsewhere without permission of the local police.

In January 1945, Hil changed jobs. He did not care for what he did at the mill and found employment at a textile factory in Leobschütz, which was much closer to Alexandra, allowing him to visit her often. He kept the factory machinery in order. Women in the area would bring him cooking vessels and various items to repair, paying with prepared food or fresh fruit. The two of them were no longer hungry. Since Hil had a satisfactory identity document, he only had to obtain proof of employment: the first certificate, dated October 21, 1944, in Bauerwitz, states he is an employee at the potato flour mill; the second, dated January 10, 1945, says he works at Josef Mutke's textile factory in Leobschütz. This document bears the notation, "Heil Hitler!"

In March, the Russian front began to draw closer. Bombs could be heard as well as the sound of cannons and Allied planes. Alexandra had to give up her room to Germans who arrived to reinforce the troops already in the area. The military ordered the civilian population to leave, saying that since the Russians were likely to kill them and rape the women, it would be better to fall into the hands of the Americans. All the Germans in the city obeyed. The farm family left and Alexandra never heard of them again.

Hil went to the farm with a Polish coworker and told Alexandra that regardless of the order, they should not leave the city: "We are close to the Polish border, we want to return home. If we go deeper into Germany, with the constant bombings we will run great risks, and besides that there will be no food. We will hide here and when the Russians enter, we will go back to Poland." As usual, his instinct led them to the path of safety.

My mother told us that while people were leaving town in wagons, on bicycles, and on horseback, the three of them – she, my father, and the Polish worker – were heading in the opposite direction, toward the city. When asked why, they said they were going to take the train. Leobschütz was deserted. The three of them hid in the factory where Hil had been working. One day, wanting a cup of coffee, he lit a fire in the kitchen. The Russians spotted the smoke from the chimney and bombed the place. Fortunately, everyone escaped unharmed. They fled to a house next to the factory, which had apparently belonged to the director because it was full of valuable objects such as fine china, liqueurs, and an abundance of food. The dwelling seemed to have been abandoned in a hurry – the table was set as if the occupants had been there only moments before. There, the three of them hid for eight days until the Russians arrived on March 25, 1945. At one point they stepped out into the street and saw others who had disobeyed the evacuation order. Russians, Poles, and Czechs who wanted to return to their countries toward the east were also hiding in that area, awaiting the arrival of the liberating army. Alexandra took some clothes from the house, also a supply of food, and it was time to depart.

On the streets the Russians ordered them to get out of there immediately because civilians could not stay at the frontlines. Off they went but not before a Russians stole Alexandra's watch. They traveled east and eventually found themselves in an area with other foreigners who had been working in Germany, all of whom were trying to find a way back to their own countries. Before letting anyone go, the Russians subjected them to lengthy interrogations, asking questions such as: "What were you doing in Germany? Where are you from? What do you want to do?" And that was just the beginning. Hil and Alexandra certainly saw this as a risk. Calculating their next move, Hill decided that they should admit to being Jews. They had to weigh their options, of which they had few. Upon receiving this information, the Russian officials immediately sent them to a makeshift office where the *NKVD* (Secret Police) had set up a control point. It was wrong to have thought things would go better if they admitted to being Jews when showing their documents. The incredulous NKVD agents replied, "You must be spies because Hitler killed all the Jews!" The agents accused them of being collaborators since it did not seem believable that any Jew could have been working freely in Germany. The agents wanted to detain them along with some Germans and a group of Ukrainian collaborators who had recently been caught. Faced with this serious situation, Hil acted wisely, approaching a heavily decorated Polish officer, and speaking to him in his language. Hil told him they were Polish, too, that they had been working in Germany and now wanted to go back home, adding that he did not understand why they were being put with the Ukrainians. The officer examined their papers which identified them as Poles, and he let them go.

Hil and Alexandra covered the 70 kilometers to the Polish border on foot. During the trek many military vehicles passed by, not one stopping to help them. A civilian offered a ride and took them a fair distance. After letting them out he sped away with their few belongings. A little further on, encountering a Russian colonel who turned out be Jewish, they identified themselves as Jews too. The Russian tried to talk to them in Yiddish. Alexandra was unable to answer. "Why do you not speak Yiddish?" he asked. She had refrained from using it for so many years that now she could not utter a single word. "I cannot say a thing, but if you give me a pencil and paper, I will write something." She jotted down a few Yiddish words and the officer was convinced. He treated them well, taking them to a farmer's house to rest for a while. After a couple of days, they went on, finally reaching the Polish border.

The war was not over even if all of Poland had been liberated. When they crossed the border at Gliwice (a Polish city adjacent to Upper Silesia), the officials gave them a certificate allowing them to travel by train anywhere in the country. Hil was still using his false name, Henryk Gajda.

Their first stopover was Łódź where they found no one they knew. Right away they observed that the violent Polish antisemitism of prewar days was as present as before, given a boost by the savage cruelty with which the Nazis had treated Jews. News was circulating of aggressions and murders. Survivors began to use the greeting *amcha* ("our people" or "our folk") to identify themselves when encountering someone who appeared to be a fellow Jew. Those still alive were free for the first time in five years and could go anywhere but felt abandoned and totally lost.

The harsh experiences of the war had created an almost indissoluble bond between Hil and Alexandra. During the 18 months they had shared, supporting each other at every moment, Alexandra saw Hil as her savior and felt very safe at his side. And for his part, Hil looked at this beautiful young woman as the only link to his family and his past. Having her with him gave meaning to his existence and he wanted to go on keeping her out of danger. They sought refuge in each other and made the decision to begin a new stage together. After several years of being robbed of their humanity, a glimmer of hope was now shining through. The possibility of leading a normal existence and starting a family was now open to them. The path was clear and deciding to take it, the couple was married in Łódź on

March 31, 1945, in a ceremony with a Jew officiating and two witnesses present.

Going on to Lublin, once again they did not run into anyone from their own city and decided it was time to return to Włodawa. En route to the station they came across two young women riding in a horse-drawn carriage, whose faces were familiar from before the war. Waving down the girls' driver, Hil and Alexandra jumped in with them and hugs and kisses were exchanged. While we do not know exactly who the young women were, we do know that there was such joy at this meeting that the driver was sure they were all related. These girls had survived in partisan brigades and knew about the events in Włodawa and nearby places. The couple was invited to spend some time with the women in their apartment in Lublin, to hear about what had happened in their town. Hil and Alexandra spent two days there, listening to the news of the annihilation of the Jews of Włodawa and the fate of those who had survived and returned to the city. With everything they learned, they found themselves facing the fact that they could well be the only survivors of their immediate families. I do not think my father ever harbored any illusion that he might come upon any family members, since he was present during the final roundups in which the Nazis had exterminated nearly all the Jews. But my mother always held a faint hope: "I knew I no longer had a family. Deep inside, I had the feeling that maybe someone had survived. I held onto that hope, and that is why we returned."

The date of their arrival in Włodawa is uncertain. In his testimony, many years later, my father mentioned that it was in May. Because they traveled so rapidly it would seem they arrived before then. There are various documents placing them in Włodawa on March 30, 1945. However, that cannot be the real date, considering that they were liberated on March 24 and had to go a considerable distance from Germany to reach their city. I suspect there was a reason for not recording the correct date. We have a document from the Włodawa City Council, dated March 30, which served as a temporary identity card and residence permit for the two of them, and another from

April 15, in which Alexandra is registered again, this time under her married name.

The couple went to the Grunhaus home on Wyrykowska Street. They found it occupied by a Pole, whom Hil knew. The man agreed they could move in. Many of the family's personal belongings were still there but my father took away only the photos, which are all we have now. Being in his home, surrounded by family possessions, with his loved ones no longer there, must have torn at his heartstrings. Surely that is when he first became conscious of the magnitude of his tragedy. He was never the same again. Although he busied himself with the daily problems he encountered, deep down he felt destroyed. My mother never said whether she went to visit her own house again.

Coming back to the city was also depressing for my mother who said that after the liberation, intense feelings of guilt began to surface: "I escaped alive, why did no one else in my family? How was that possible? While you were living day by day during the war, you did not give it much thought, you would receive a harsh blow and you just went on ahead. It must have been the survival instinct. I never suspected something such as that was going to happen, then once I was free, for a long time I could not speak of the losses. I could not bear knowing I was the only survivor. It was terrible." She said over and over that she was luckier than her siblings since someone was always taking care of her: "Esther and then Hil made the decisions that saved me."

The war ended in May 1945 and those who had gone to the Soviet Union began returning home – Sara and her husband Misha Omelinski, Yehezkel Huberman, Alexandra's first cousin Yankele Lederman and his wife Hashe, among others – all of them hoping to find some friend or relative alive. Alexandra and Sara's reunion was quite emotional, a mixture of happiness and great sadness. When they separated in 1943, they had promised to meet again and remain as sisters if they survived, and here were the two of them, who had done just that.

Sara and Alexandra in Włodawa

They all moved into a house belonging to Sara's uncle, on a kind of farm or kibbutz as Sara called it. Hil and Sara's husband, Misha, became good friends, playing poker at night and walking a lot during the day. In photos from that time, taken on the outskirts of Włodawa, Alexandra has a smile, and all the women look pretty and well dressed. These pictures attest to special, happy moments shared in a kind of rebirth despite the many sad memories.

To support themselves and eat – as my mother put it – on July 17 she closed the sale of her inheritance: a family house and the shops of her father and grandfather in the rynek. She did not get much money for those properties. In June, Hil went to Gdynia to see the sawmill and the house he owned and decide what to do with them. The sawmill was completely cleared out; all the machinery had been taken, as well as the wood. He managed to sell his property, and meanwhile, had to plan how he could work for a living. He also sold what the family owned in Włodawa: his parents' house, his brother Leo's house (both on Wyrykowska Street), and a 7,900-square-foot lot on Solna Street. In forms they later filled out for the International Red Cross, the couple declared they were in Włodawa until the end of July and in August moved to Gdynia. Hil worked there for several months, most likely in the lumber trade, which he knew well. He also made a trip to Warsaw to see Zielinski, who had some of his gold coins, but it turned out the dentist had died during the bombings.

Poland continued to be quite dangerous for Jews. The survivors, stunned, wondered how it was possible for so much antisemitism to still exist. Fed on Nazi propaganda, many Poles had actively participated in the betrayal and persecution of Jews or had looked on without protest, permitting the annihilation of their fellow citizens. Those Poles who had benefited from the disappearance of the Jews by appropriating their assets, began to see Jews returning at the war's end and feared they would be required to give everything back. This greatly increased hostility toward the returnees or, at best, led to indifference.

Alexandra, Hil, Sara, Misha with friends in Włodawa

By and large, most Jews were unaware of the magnitude of the catastrophe that had devastated Polish Jewry. Only ten percent had survived. For those left, it was impossible to contemplate rebuilding a future there when they had lost their families and their communities no longer existed.

The government welcomed the returning Jews officially, granting them equal rights. This, however, was not reflected in the mood of the forces of order; members of the AK were still actively persecuting Jewish survivors. The situation grew more serious by the day, from attacks on trains bringing Jews out of the Soviet Union, to murders on the street and assaults on the synagogues still in use. Once again, Jews felt threatened. On August 11, 1945, the unimaginable happened: a pogrom in Krakow, instigated by false rumors that Jews had killed Polish children in a ritual murder at the Kupa Synagogue, which was subsequently attacked by a mob of young thugs supported by the militia and Polish soldiers. There were five deaths and many injuries.

The Krakow pogrom more than alarmed the Jews left in Poland, and those in Włodawa acquired weapons to protect themselves; most of them were ex-partisans and knew how to use guns. No incidents were reported in Włodawa proper, but many began to feel threatened because in nearby towns some returning Jews had been murdered. Confronted with this situation, the Polish government took some measures, encouraging Jews to settle in certain locations, such as Szczecin, which had been recovered in 1945. A city on the Baltic Sea, it seemed a safe refuge for Jews. The Germans living there had been forced to leave, and not many Poles remained. The authorities provided housing and business opportunities so those who relocated there could support themselves. Sara, her husband, and their whole group of friends left for Szczecin in September of that year.

Alexandra was not happy in Gdynia. She had no friends and spent her days alone, which added to her depression, so she and Hil decided she would move to Szczecin. The change did her good. The couple rented a furnished apartment in the building where their friends had settled and Hil visited on weekends. The living quarters were quite comfortable and were grouped around a central courtyard. By now, Alexandra was pregnant, and Hil brought a woman named Jadwiga from Gdynia to help her with the housework. The atmosphere of the city was not always pleasant. During the day, Alexandra and Sara and their friends went out walking but they did not dare leave home at night. The town was full of heavy-drinking Russians who were known to become aggressive when inebriated.

With a communist government looming in Poland, Hil and Alexandra planned to leave the country as soon as possible. As my father later recalled: "We returned to Włodawa and found no one alive, we no longer had any family. My father's sawmill was on the other side of the Bug, in Soviet territory, so we no longer had a means of livelihood. So what did we have to seek there? My parents' house? Besides, the communists had already arrived, and we did not want to settle among them. It was better to leave." Many of the survivors who had returned to Włodawa felt the same way: in September 1945 there were 143 Jews in the city; in 1946 only 40; in 1947 just 5; and in 1948 only 3. And the same thing happened in the rest of Poland: of the approximately 350,000 Jews who survived, 40,000 to 50,000 left the country between July and October 1945. By September 1946, 100,000 more had departed.

In 1945, the borders were still mostly open. The first time Hil and Alexandra tried to cross to the American side, however, they failed. Since Alexandra was in the last stages of her pregnancy with me, they had to wait until after my birth to try again. I was born January 31, 1946, and my parents named me Yanet Pnina. Yanet was not a Jewish name but was selected because of the circumstances of the moment. Pnina was for Perla, my maternal grandmother. Right after my birth, they began planning how they could escape from Poland once it was a little warmer. Their moment came in the middle of March, when I was six weeks old. They paid a Russian soldier who had a truck with a closed cab to take them across the border to Berlin. The soldier put his cloak around my mother, who was holding me, and she sat up front with him as if she were his wife. When someone spoke to them, she would merely smile. My father hid in the back, among the boxes being transported. They did not search the truck at the border, so we got through without a problem. I behaved well and did not cry. My mother talked about this journey many times, laughing: "Just imagine, there I sat, not knowing a word of Russian and wondering what I was going to say if they spoke to me, so I laughed the whole time. I was frightened, yet it all turned out fine." We arrived in Berlin on March 24, 1946, and went to Schlachtensee, a displaced persons camp, run by the United Nations Relief and Rehabilitation Administration (UNRRA) and the Americans. There we encountered people from many nations who had fled from communism taking root in countries liberated by the Soviet Union. My mother appreciated how well organized the camp was. The three of us were registered and given identity cards which allowed us to obtain monthly ration cards and any other necessary items. They found us living quarters and provided all the milk I needed. My mother knew this was a place of transit for refugees, yet we were all treated well and had enough to eat. We stayed until May 30, 1946.

At first my parents anticipated emigrating to Palestine. In the registration records from Schlachtensee that was listed as our destination. But my father had serious doubts because he did not accept the idea of our being illegal immigrants, which is how we would have been classified upon arrival there. In the meantime, there began a worldwide distribution of lists of survivors, and those who had living friends or relatives tried to get in touch with them. My parents had registered with the Central Committee of Polish Jews (*CKZP*) while still in Lublin and because of that received letters from friends in Argentina and the United States offering them help to emigrate. My father had a good friend from Włodawa living in Denver, Colorado. The idea of settling in the United States did not appeal to him, nor did Argentina seem like the right option. But then an opportunity came through a man named Leon Sznajderman, originally from Włodawa, who got us visas to travel to Venezuela. Sznajderman had settled there before the war. He was grateful to my father, who had helped him so he could go to Caracas where he was now living quite happily and doing well financially. Venezuela was a great unknown to us, as my father said later: "Venezuela? Where is that? What is it like?" My parents tried to find basic information: work opportunities, living conditions, what sort of country it was. They heard only that Caracas had a splendid climate, an eternal spring. Sznajderman kept writing and offered to work with my parents on all the documents needed for the trip. So we changed course; our little family would be heading to Venezuela.

Preparations for the trip went quickly. Many organizations gave support to displaced persons. From Berlin we went on to Frankfort where, on August 2, the Office of Military Government of the American Zone in Germany issued an identity document which served as a passport for the three of us. There are some old snapshots of my mother that were taken during those days spent in Germany: one shows her taking me for an outing in Berlin; in another, from Frankfort, she is in the countryside with a friend, standing before a horse-drawn cart. In every photo from this time period she is smiling broadly.

Our last stop in Germany was to spend a few days at a displaced persons camp in Munich. There we registered with the Joint, which took care of displaced persons. They guided us through the process of preparing for immigration to Venezuela and they paid our expenses. On August 27, we left with a safe-conduct credential stamped at the bottom of our identity document, authorizing us to make a single journey, to Paris.

My mother and me in Berlin

Frankfurt, August 1946

Munich, August 1946

By August 28 we were in France. We received identity cards for foreigners, valid through October 11, and renewed twice up until December 11. We also obtained a residence permit. Since Włodawa, my father had taken back his real name, with a slight spelling change: Hil Grunhaus. My mother opted to keep the first name from her false papers, and to use both her maiden name and her married name: Alexandra Lederman Grunhaus. As for me, the spelling of my name, Yanet, was changed in Paris. It was either my parents or the French authorities who were responsible for my becoming Jeannette.

Our quarters at 62 Rue Roquette were in the 11th arrondissement. As rationing was in force, each time Joint gave us milk, it was noted on our letter of safe-conduct, which was our passport and our key to survival. My mother never talked about those three months in Paris. We have some snapshots in which she looks happy going about the city, in front of the Eiffel Tower, and at the gardens of Chaillot. These attest to the beginning of a new existence.

Mother in Paris, September 1946

Mother in Paris, September 1946

Leon Sznajderman sent us our tickets for Venezuela, and on November 12, 1946, we set sail at Le Havre on the SS Columbia, en route to La Guaira. My father often talked about how he exchanged our first-class tickets for economy berths so as "to have something in my pocket." Jews were not allowed into Venezuela at the time, so we were to be listed as Catholics or Protestants. Joint handled the processing of the documents we would need to embark.

The crossing, which lasted about two weeks, was especially hard for my mother, who was seasick and ate virtually nothing. My father took care of me. I was already eight months old and a seasoned traveler. I behaved well and did not get sick, which allowed him to carry me around the ship and meet other refugees going to La Guaira and socialize with them. We docked on November 26. My father used to say he arrived in Venezuela with me, a Leica (his camera), and 70 dollars. A totally unfamiliar panorama awaited us in this new land. We disembarked full of uncertainty but with great hope.

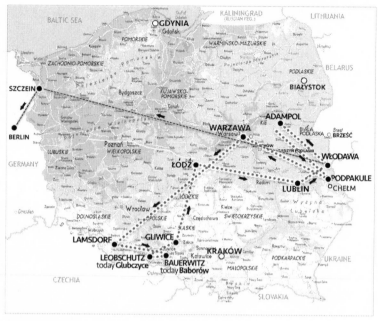

Wlodawa - Adampol/Natalin - Podpakule - Warsaw - Lamsdorf - Bauerwitz (today Baborów) -
Leobschutz (today Glubzyce) - Gliwice (where they crossed the border to return to Poland) -
Lodz - Lublin - Wlodawa

Wlodawa - Szczecin - Berlin - Frankfort - Munich - Paris - Caracas, Venezuela - Maracaibo

13

VENEZUELA: A NEW LIFE

As we disembarked, my parents' first moments in their new country surely must have astonished them. They stepped out into a bustling and disorderly port, with people of many races speaking an unknown and incomprehensible language, brightly colored little buildings – and heat, great heat.

At the end of the road that climbed to Caracas, there appeared before our eyes a beautiful landscape. We were looking at a picturesque city of red roofs, built in a valley at the foot of a spectacular, imposing mountain range, with luxurious vegetation, and a profusion of flowers. A temperate climate heralded an eternal spring, just as my parents had been told in Europe. Leon and Clara Sznajderman welcomed us warmly into their house for a couple of weeks, before we moved into the modest apartment they had rented for us.

Leon had emigrated to Venezuela in 1932. In 1937, he returned to Poland to marry, as did many Jews. Once back in Caracas, he opened a fur shop. By 1946, he was quite well established, also owning some other businesses. My father was going to work in one of them as a start. Since he did not speak Spanish, when Leon took him to one of the shops, he could only stand by and observe. This did not seem to work out, and the two men agreed that he absolutely had to pick up some Spanish. But deep down, being an employee seemed out of place to my father, since he had always been the boss, running things and giving orders. Fortunately, another opportunity soon arose.

Managing to work around the restrictions on Jewish immigration, many survivors of the war were arriving in Caracas and warmly received by the Jewish community, which assisted them in finding housing and work. Right away my parents began meeting other Jews, my father telling them about his background in the lumber industry.

In December, Lazaro Levine – a Jewish gentleman from Maracaibo – visited Caracas. He owned a furniture factory and had a sawmill that was losing money because it was not run efficiently. A mutual friend told Levine, "Look, a fellow has just arrived from Poland who says he is an expert in lumber and running sawmills. Hire him temporarily and see how it turns out." Levine met with my father to inquire about his background in the lumber trade, to which my father said: "I know all there is to know about the wood industry. Obviously, the types of wood are not the same here but that will not be a problem for me." They reached an agreement for a one-month trial with the possibility of a future contract. My mother and I stayed in Caracas while my father went off to Maracaibo. He more than lived up to Mr. Levine's expectations, and a month later they signed a one-year contract that named Hil as the company's manager. My mother and I arrived in Maracaibo in March 1947. As always, my father had chosen the path that seemed the most feasible for our family, with this new city offering the best opportunity.

Maracaibo, on the western shore of the lake with same name, is Venezuela's second largest city and in 1946 had a population of 200,000. Some 703 kilometers from Caracas and rather isolated from the rest of the country, the city was accessible only by air or ferry. The eastern shore was rich in oil fields, and many petroleum exploration and drilling companies had been established in the area.

My father, who spoke three languages, had to quickly apply himself to acquire the basic Spanish he needed to communicate with his workers or else he would not have been able to do his job. To get things done to his liking he had to change almost his entire crew and train them accordingly. The first few months were certainly hard. He was in an environment unlike anything he had experienced before, with a language barrier and a completely different working style. In addition, the unmerciful Maracaibo sun was a great challenge for him. My mother often told us how our fair-skinned father would come home from work sunburned but quite happy. Three months in, the sawmill was already showing such an increase in earnings that once the first contract had ended, another was offered, entitling him to a percentage of the profits. From the beginning, he knew how to run the firm and establish contacts with foreign companies that had branches in Venezuela, these becoming his best clients.

When my mother and I arrived in Maracaibo my father had already found us a place to stay, rented from one of the Jews living in the city. My mother described it as an old house with high ceilings and a thatched roof. It had two parts: the front included the living room and bedrooms; in the back was the kitchen. They were joined by a long-roofed walkway which opened to the outside. The patio sat below street level and during Maracaibo's frequent heavy rains it would flood, and the neighbors' children would come over to sail their paper boats. Such scenes make up some of my earliest recollections: me, at age four, having a good time splashing in the water.

Although I was used to traveling, as soon as we arrived in Maracaibo, I became ill, probably because of the change in climate and diet. I do not know whether my mother was aware when we left Caracas' temperate zone, with its average temperature of 68ºF, that we were entering a region where it was around 104ºF during the hottest months. This was a shock for both of us, and we could not handle the heat. In my mother's words, "It was horrible! The heat was oppressive, I had no appetite, I lost weight, I was exhausted, and I thought constantly about how to get out of there." It was all very hard on her. She improved somewhat after my father bought her a fan. As for me, just learning to walk, I began getting blisters which would burst and become infected and there were many visits to a clinic for antibiotics. The doctor finally recommended a trip to a temperate zone as a cure. So, my mother and I spent a month and a half in the cooler climate of the Venezuelan Andes, in the little village of La Mesa de Esnujaque. I got better and trips to La Mesa later became a treasured vacation destination.

The community in Maracaibo was made up of Ashkenazi and Sephardic Jews. The Sephardim (from Arab countries and Palestine) were the first Jews to arrive in the region, coming between the end of the 19th century and the first years of the 20th century. The Ashkenazi (from eastern Europe) began arriving in the 1920s and 1930s. By 1944, the local Jews had created La Sociedad Israelita de Maracaibo, a community institution still functioning today. When my parents arrived, the "Sociedad," was well established.

And the first years passed. My mother soon learned Spanish, speaking it quite well, with just a slight accent. She used Yiddish or Spanish with my father, never Polish, and Spanish with us children. From the time we arrived in Venezuela, my father took the name Enrique, the Spanish version of his birth name, Chil, while my mother went on being Alexandra (pronouncing it *Alejandra),* her Polish friends still calling her *Sheindele.* My father called her Olesh, for Olesia, the Polish diminutive of Alexandra. She called him Geñek, Polish for Enrique. I never asked my mother why she decided to change her name for good. I can only speculate that she kept Alexandra because it was easy to say in Spanish. Or more significantly, perhaps it had to do with the inner struggle that had begun while she was still in Europe: on the one hand, she was adapting to the person she became after the war; on the other, she was unable to make a break with her past or deal with her losses.

My parents fit into the community with ease. They rarely referred to their history, and when new friends asked them about it, my mother never wanted to say anything. Like many other survivors, the two of them had endured events so traumatic that those who had not experienced them would not comprehend the true dimension of their suffering. Few survivors ended up in Maracaibo; most of those who made their way to Venezuela settled in Caracas.

Our family continued to adapt smoothly to the society and the community, and life was very peaceful. My mother talked about walking me to a little square nearby where she met other mothers and grandmothers. By coincidence, my future husband, Rafael Gelman, used to spend afternoons there with his grandmother, never imagining what the years held in store for us. Rafael and I knew each other from childhood and were neighbors a little later, which led to close ties between our two families, with a standing invitation to share each other's religious and social celebrations.

Before long I had a baby brother. Leon Jacob Moses was born in 1948 and named in honor of our two grandfathers and my father's brother. My mother was not sure what we should call him. It was my father who chose: "Simply Leo." It was a symbolic counterpoint between recollections of a past which resurfaced with the names of those who came before, and a present filled with hope and possibilities for the family newly formed.

Because my mother could not bear the oppressive climate, in 1950 my father went to Israel to explore the possibility of our emigrating there. The State of Israel had been created in 1948. In 1950 the new country was undergoing constant struggles, and war with the Arabs was on the horizon. In the face of all the advice from relatives and acquaintances, my father decided we would stay where we were for the time being. The idea of moving to another city was a familiar subject of debate in our household. Since my parents never agreed about the matter, Maracaibo became our home for almost the rest of our lives. When he came back from Israel my father continued in the work he knew best: the lumber business. And with the advent of air conditioning in the early fifties, my mother's daily suffering changed radically: she went from the constant torment of the oppressive heat to feeling great relief in a cool house and, thus, her days became much more enjoyable.

Our family was growing. In 1956, almost ten years after we arrived in Venezuela, my sister Rosa Esther was born, named for my paternal grandmother and my mother's sister. It was a moment of great joy – there was one more of us. Devoted to their young family, my parents focused their energies on creating a stable home for us while also participating actively in the events of the community. As my mother recalled:

> The community was nice and the people congenial. We soon started joining in all their activities. Since most of them had come from Europe, we all wanted to be together, and we established a club on a lot with an old, old house. We made the one living room into a synagogue, with most activities taking place outdoors on the earthen patio or the terrace. We would meet there Saturdays, Sundays, and other nights of the week. We would chat, play cards, hear lectures ... All the children came, they played, watched movies. It was an ugly place, yet everyone, the kids especially, liked it because their friends were there.

Programs for Hanukkah, Purim, and Shavuot took place on the terrace. There was no Jewish school then, so the ladies of the community took on the task of offering classes for children and preparing with them performances for each holiday. We all took part and joined in enthusiastically. On weekends sometimes several families would take the ferry and cross to the other side of the lake, but we did not get off. My mother loved those boat rides. It was a change of scenery, and she enjoyed the breeze over the water, the new smells and sensations, and chats with her friends. "The trip was so pleasant and pretty," she used to remark. Another regular activity consisted of excursions to beaches on the lake, which in those days was not polluted. We could bathe and swim to our heart's content while the grownups took care of the food and played cards or took a dip in the water.

During school vacations, my mother and many other friends from the Jewish community moved to La Mesa de Esnujaque with their children. Back then it was a long trip. We had to cross the lake on the ferry and then drive for several hours on rather primitive winding roads. These holidays lasted several weeks. On the weekends the men arrived loaded with provisions, since the food served in the local hotels was not too satisfactory. With the town standing on a plain at an altitude of 1742 meters, the cool – and even cold – nights delighted us summer visitors. We children had a really good time. We took walks together, go down to the river, ride horseback, pick blackberries (just as my mother did as a girl in Włodawa), or visit nearby villages. The adults entertained themselves by chatting and playing cards. These trips reminded my mother of Europe: the climate, the vegetation, walking through the woods. Those were such pleasant interludes!

My mother was happy during these first years in Maracaibo. My parents went out every evening, enjoying their circle of close friends. To one place one day, another the next. "We would get in the car and driving by a friend's house, if we saw cars we would stop on the spur of the moment, knowing that another day our house would be the meeting place." In a way these friendships turned into our family group. Since all they had known was now gone, at the outset my parents drew special sustenance from the links formed with members of their Jewish community. "We all made contacts with Venezuelans from different backgrounds. We joined charitable organizations in Maracaibo's society and in other parts of the country, yet our closest circle consisted of our Jewish friends."

The difficult postwar road, with the clear realization that they were alone, led my parents to put all their effort into going forward and rebuilding their lives. They had to bury their past for a few years as they concentrated on forming a new family. This must have seemed like almost a sacred obligation to them, since it was the only way to rise above the Holocaust. Fighting to restore a sense of normalcy involved a monumental effort.

During the economic boom, the community's situation – and with it, our family's – became more and more organized. The year 1953 saw the founding of a Spanish Hebrew school, the Colegio Hispano-Hebreo Bilú. In 1961–1962, a new community center (commonly called "the club") was built: the home of two synagogues, one Ashkenazi and the other Sephardic. There also sprang up a network of community institutions like the ones that already existed in Caracas. At its height, Maracaibo's Jewish community included some 120 families. There were regular contacts between the Maracaibo and Caracas groups – with cultural, athletic, and social exchanges among the adults (and more so among the young people) – under the auspices of Maccabi Hatzair, the Young Zionist Movement.

Maracaibo was developing rapidly and began offering a variety of cultural options. My parents especially liked taking us children to concerts by internationally famed musicians. Arthur Rubinstein, Yehudi Menuhin, and the New York Philharmonic led by Leonard Bernstein, were just some of the concerts we attended. The Teatro Baralt, the site of many of these performances, had been in existence since 1896. There was also the Universidad del Zulia, established in 1891 and reopened in 1946, an academic and cultural center of the highest quality.

The city welcomed newcomers. From the first my family had a good reception. My mother used to say that the people of Maracaibo were generous and caring, albeit lively, and maybe even a bit rowdy but noble at heart. There were a fair number of immigrants from the Middle East, called "Turcos (Turks)," including the Jews. They did not suffer any kind of discrimination. The community established close ties with the civil, religious, and legal authorities of the city. Figures from local government such as the city's governor and leaders of the Catholic Church, were often invited to Jewish social festivities, most notably to Israel's Independence Day celebrations.

In Venezuela my father continued guiding us on the road of life. He was the central figure in our family – honest, strong, decisive, and at the same time, our protector. He changed greatly after the war destroyed his spirit. Of that cheerful young jokester described by Michael Garin, there remained only a few traces that would sometimes surface on festive occasions. Generally, in my memory, he stands out as rather serious, quite intellectual, and interested in national and international political issues, especially regarding Israel. He was an omnivorous reader: newspapers (to stay informed about happenings in the world), plus literary works of all kinds. He held firm opinions, never hesitating to express them quite forcefully. The community respected him and considered him a wise person. Many of my brother Leo's friends admired our father, valued his advice, and often went to him with problems they were facing. He also enjoyed playing chess and on weekends would frequently seek out opponents at the local community center. His passionate defense of the State of Israel was his most outstanding characteristic. The Zionist ideals instilled in him early by his father were reinforced over time and passed down to the next generation. And they are one of the beacons that guides our family to this day.

My mother, totally devoted to her children, had a strong sense of morality and honor. Her example taught us how to distinguish good from evil. She was a kindhearted person, always ready to help those in need. Although she was rather anxious, I never felt even a touch of overprotection. She was pretty with her dark hair, fair skin, and sweet expression. Those looks never gave rise to vanity – to her, beauty was of no importance. From the time I was a child, I saw a deep sadness in her. When cheerful on some happy occasion, she would merely smile rather than laugh. She was shy and somewhat quiet but made friends easily. Brought up with traditional ideas, it was hard for her to accept change. Reading was a favorite activity for her, and like my father, that also meant keeping abreast of current political events, especially those concerning Israel. A committed Zionist who loved Israel, no one was allowed to criticize it in her presence. She was an excellent cook and enjoyed preparing all kinds of dishes that her grandchildren recall to this day with delight. Her Apfelstrudel, chicken schnitzel and coffee cake are some of the specialties that have now become treasured family recipes.

We always knew how much our parents loved us. They showed it in their attitudes and their actions, even though they did not readily express it and were not much given to physical shows of affection. I always knew, however, that their existence centered on us. We could see their pride in our achievements, especially when they mentioned them to other people.

As one would expect, my parents tried to follow the values that had made up the universe of their childhood and youth. My father honored the example of his father, Jacob – a generous, compassionate man and a Zionist who was devoted to his community. From an early age my father had felt that paternal influence, which led to his own involvement with Włodawa's community institutions. In Maracaibo he continued his efforts to help society, participating in the founding of the Colegio Hispano-Hebreo Bilú. He was also active in organizations like the Keren Kayemet LeIsrael, for which he had served as secretary during his younger days in Poland. He worked with Keren Hayesod, a group that raised money to help the State of Israel, and with B'nai B'rith, an international humanitarian aid group fighting racism and xenophobia. In the 1970s, he spent eight years as the head of the board of directors of the Sociedad Israelita de Maracaibo. He always considered his most important accomplishment as chairman to be his collaboration with the Jewish Agency of Caracas to help some 12 people – children and adults – emigrate to Israel. That success brought him great satisfaction.

Both he and my mother welcomed the creation of a Hebrew school in Maracaibo. My mother spoke proudly of my father's part in that project, and I am sure she found a parallel with what her father, Moses, did in establishing the Beit Yaakov school in Włodawa. In the introduction of Jewish schooling in Maracaibo she saw her father's legacy carried on. Both my parents were intelligent people who kept close watch over our studies. From the time we were small, my mother saw to it that we did our schoolwork. Education held a high place in our household, our parents quite demanding in this respect. Since neither of them had been given the opportunity for higher education, without undue pressure they instilled in us the desire to prepare for professional careers and we understood they expected us to receive degrees. And that is what the three of us did, each one in a different field.

As we became more economically secure, our parents could afford to do more for us and we started to travel outside Venezuela – first to the United States, then quite often to Israel. Our initial visit to the US was to see my mother's cousin Yankele Lederman, his wife Hashe, and their children. Later, we embarked on seasonal visits to Miami. While we children were learning English at summer camp and enjoying vacation activities, my parents were becoming acquainted with people, mostly Jewish, from other Latin American countries. Friends from Venezuela would also come to Miami, and my parents would get together with them to enjoy the pleasures of the city. In the Miami Beach of the 1960s, Jews could easily find little restaurants serving typical Jewish cuisine, stores selling traditional Jewish foods, and small shops owned by Jews with whom one could speak Yiddish. There were also plays and musicals in Yiddish which allowed my parents to briefly relive the world they had lost, and those moments delighted them.

Their favorite place to visit, however, was Israel. My parents had an unconditional devotion to that country. To them, it was an overwhelming affirmation of survival. They loved being there. Often they would get together with my father's second cousin, Michael Garin, who in 1939 became the first in the family to emigrate to Israel. Sara, his mother, his brother Marian (who had emigrated after the war), also visited them. Close friends, for example Ziche Fuchs, who had traveled to Palestine with Hil in 1924, and others came as well, many of them survivors from Włodawa. I still visualize those reunions as one big party, joyful and emotional. Usually they spoke Yiddish or Polish, sharing their memories, telling their stories once more. Hearing Polish made a strong and lasting impression on me, but it was not a positive one. I rejected the idea of trying to learn the language – it did not interest me. On these trips our parents were truly happy. The family went on many excursions and together we visited all of Israel. My father enjoyed walking the area around Rothschild Street. Familiar to him from his days in Palestine in the

'20s, the neighborhood brought back pleasant memories of his youth. For my mother, the most important and gratifying part of those visits was seeing her soul sister, Sara. Since their parting in 1946 they had stayed permanently in touch, and their mutual affection never stopped growing. It was not just a shared past that made them close, for now they were sharing their present. During our visits, they spent time together constantly – either with family or just the two of them – and they never stopped talking. For both, having their children beside them represented continuity. Despite adversity, they had managed to build a different world, one that was strong and stable.

Both my parents came from Orthodox families. My father's family was somewhat more liberal, but most definitely Orthodox. In Maracaibo, with such a small number of Jewish families, it was difficult to maintain the pattern of religious practices that they had been forced to abandon during the war. Doing so did not seem all that important to my father, but it was vital to him to identify with Judaism through its values and traditions and pass those on to his children. From our early days, we were made to feel proud of our Jewish heritage, and a love for Israel was a constant in our household. I shall never forget our happy Shabbat celebrations and all the holidays when my mother would fill the house with guests, treating them to her culinary specialties.

My mother was basically in agreement with my father's outlook, though as the years went by, she began to have an inner conflict. She could not forget the teachings of Moses, her father. To her, a closed society like that of Włodawa made it possible for Jews to preserve their identity. She idealized such a way of life, often saying, "In Poland the Jews kept to themselves as if in a ghetto, they were not open to the outside world. I am firmly convinced this is what kept them from disappearing. They guarded their traditions and did not become assimilated." She saw that as positive and never allowed us to argue about the matter or try to show her there were other aspects – maybe even some negative ones – to the dynamic of a closed society. Missing deeply the world of her childhood and youth, she had locked it in her memory like a treasure and it could not compare with anything that came after.

Much later I was surprised when my sister Rosa told me our mother had suffered from a major internal struggle with God. She had talked about it with Rosa, but not with me. I am not sure whether she lost her faith completely, but I learned that she had far-reaching doubts. The foundation of her beliefs seemed to have been destroyed. What was the purpose of God? What determined good and evil? For God, what was life worth? And, above all, who was this God who allowed his people to confront such tragedy during the Holocaust? She asked Rosa, "How can such a God exist, a God silent in the face of such monstrosities?" Whether she ever found answers to her questions or made peace with her God, I shall never know. She certainly seemed connected to her Judaism, keeping little books of psalms and Hebrew prayers on her bedside table. For a long time, my father appeared to be totally distanced from religion, although not from tradition. During his last years, however, when we would attend the synagogue, I could see a change in him. He gave the impression of being more observant than in earlier days.

Once my family had achieved a measure of stability, and my parents did not have any economic worries, the demons of the past began to resurface – with each of them reacting differently to the traumas they had lived through. I did not realize it back then, but my father was probably tortured by his memories. I am sure he missed his family a great deal, though I have no recollection of him verbalizing this. He became increasingly harsh, irritable, argumentative, and intransigent.

As for my mother, she fell into a severe clinical depression. Tormented by her survival, the image of her sister Esther plagued her day and night. The memory of the rest of her family beset her too, but foremost was that of Esther, who had offered her, the little sister, the only road to salvation. Unable to allow the profound gratitude she felt toward Esther to surface, she was overwhelmed by guilt, constantly asking herself, "Why did I survive and not her? Why?"

Like many survivors, she had repressed her sorrow, and did not allow herself enough time to deal adequately with her grief. Surely, horrible images of the war must have gone round and round in her head: the terror, the daily perils, the uncertainty, the hunger, and most of all, the loss of all her loved ones. She stopped eating, sleeping, functioning, and closed herself off from the world, taking no interest in anything. We three children and our father saw her submerge into the despair and witnessed her suffering. We tried to help her, comfort her, give her strength, but our efforts were in vain. We had no choice but to learn to cope with her struggles.

These episodes of severe depression were associated with my mother's being dissatisfied with herself. She became nervous, insecure, and more dependent. Growing bothered by social conventions that appeared false, she began to magnify some of the mores of the society in which she lived. The comparison with the standards of the world of her youth – now idealized in her mind – troubled her greatly. And yet she stayed in touch with her good friends, who were always there. For my mother it became almost lifesaving to maintain connections with her social network. After two or three critical years of relentless depression, there would be stable periods, lasting a little longer each time. It was a shaky recovery; a minor problem or worry was enough to trigger another marked decline. Dealing with the situation must have been difficult for my father as well as for my sister and brother. Rosa was a little girl and Leo was just entering his teens when they had to face the absence of a maternal figure for long stretches. I was older and better able to deal with things on my own. My mother's state made me truly sad, still I was able to carry on.

Little by little my mother began to handle her sickness. She accepted her sleeplessness and spent the wee hours of the morning listening to music to avoid negative thoughts. What helped her most was adopting a different attitude toward life, recognizing the things she could not change and being proactive in ways that helped her move on. At the same time the happy events that began unfolding around her contributed to her improvement. From 1979 on, there were only a few relapses, usually brief, thanks to the new generation of medications she agreed to take.

A day came when my father was given the opportunity to tell his story of the war years and seek justice for the losses that he, my mother, and so many had suffered. Włodawa survivors gathered annually in Israel to mourn and honor their lost loved ones. Hil would join them if he happened to be in Israel when they met. They had rebuilt their lives, yet they could not forget. In 1960 they decided to contact Yad Vashem,[1] to report on the crimes committed in Włodawa by Richard Nitschke and to request that he be found and brought to justice. That initiated a series of contacts with Germany, leading to an unexpected result: On May 4, 1961, Nitschke was arrested.

On August 15, my father received a letter from the World Jewish Congress notifying him that German lawyers were gathering information which could lead to the prosecution of the head of the Włodawa Border Police (SS Unterstürmführer), Richard Nitschke. The letter requested that my father inform them about the events he had witnessed, identify other perpetrators, and provide names of fellow survivors willing to cooperate with the investigation. My father replied quickly, on August 23, in a long document in which he summarized the requested information and stated he was willing to travel to Germany to testify.

Proceedings got underway quickly. The designated prosecutor contacted over 100 witnesses, my father among them. On June 12, 1962, through the German Embassy in Caracas, my father received his first official communication. It informed him that pending in the Hanover District Court was a criminal trial against 12 Germans, members of the "post of the Włodawa/Bug Frontier Police during the Second World War, charged with having committed numerous crimes of murder and complicity in murder." The document went on to cite dates and places, including: "from 1942 to 1943 in Włodawa and the surrounding area; in December and January of 1939–40 near Sobibor and Orchówek." As part of the preliminary investigation requested by the Hanover Regional Tribunal, on June 26, 1962, my father gave a statement at the office of the German Embassy in Caracas. Many such statements were also collected in Israel, Canada, Germany, and other countries.

In September 1963, the World Jewish Congress wrote to my father with the news that the prosecutor had issued an indictment against six Nazis. The initial 12 defendants had been reduced to 6: Nitschke and 5 of his aides, including Müller, would be tried for "their participation in the selection and deportation of at least 7,000 Jews to Sobibor and for the shooting of a number of Jews. In addition, Nitschke and Müller were accused of murdering a number of Russian Jews who were prisoners of war." Then, on March 2, 1964, the prosecutor's office of the Hanover District Court summoned my father to testify in that city on Thursday, July 30, at 8:15 a.m. Now my father faced a dilemma as to whether he should appear. On the one hand, it would be a victory for him if his testimony helped bring justice for the extermination of all his family; on the other, it would mean having to travel to Germany, and the mere idea of being near ex-Nazis made him ill. He had never wanted to return to Poland, and Germany was an even more terrible symbol of all his misfortunes. In the end, however, he decided to make the trip to take part in what he called "the tragic epilogue to the bloody history of Judaism in Włodawa."

His detailed testimony began with relating the atrocities committed against the Jews in Włodawa from 1939 until 1942. He described the persecution of Polish intellectuals and dignitaries set in motion by Nitschke, their subsequent imprisonment in Lublin and their murder at Auschwitz. Then he described the various roundups, the murder of Rabbi Leiner, and a series of individual executions, most of them carried out by Nitschke. At the end, my father wanted it entered into the record that "Nitschke never gave the Jewish Council written orders. All those who could later become witnesses were systematically taken out of play by Nitschke. After they were shot and killed, their houses were broken into and sacked."

In Hanover my father met with the other witnesses who had agreed to make the journey to testify. We have a photo showing him with Leon Lemberger, Yehezkel Huberman, Sara Omelinski, Abraham Khoine, and Tamar Turkienicz.

Hanover, July 1946 (Yizkor Book)

Bernard Falkenberg was also there, along with Franz Holtzheimer and Willy Selinger. Falkenberg did not look well. He was living in the German Democratic Republic, his economic situation precarious. They took up a collection to help him the best they could. My father and Franz Holtzheimer also signed sworn statements in his favor.[2]

Those statements were quite important for Falkenberg. In them, my father asserted he had known the man ever since his arrival in Włodawa because he used to go to the sawmill where my father worked to pick up wood supplies. "Falkenberg helped the Jews at all times. He aided them economically, kept them from being killed and warned them whenever he found out arrests were being planned." Thanks to Falkenberg my father was able to flee to Warsaw. "He provided me [with] a good document with a false name and during the fifth roundup he hid me in his bedroom until I could escape to the woods. And while I was out there, he sent me a blanket through

Zielinski, a Polish friend. Falkenberg also helped many other Jews hiding in the woods. Communication took place through messengers. His decency and his compassion for human life were what sent Falkenberg to prison and Mauthausen."[3]

In 1974, in his article for the *Yizkor Book*, my father expressed feelings I had never heard him speak aloud. He began with a moving sentence: "I am going to talk of my city as I knew it, as I always see it, as I will see it until the day I die." He went on to give a detailed description of Włodawa, recounting what happened there during the war. He referred to anti-Nazi legal action with harshness and skepticism: "In my opinion, all the so-called 'anti-Nazi trials' are orchestrated with the intention of clearing the German people of guilt and responsibility, and showing that only a few isolated Germans are guilty, and not totally, all the while taking into account that each one of the accused 'obeyed' orders given in wartime. Trials are set up, [and] ridiculous punishments are handed out [as a means] to show that it is not the German people who are at fault for the extermination of six million Jews." He confessed that "in the days before and after [his] testifying, [he] relived the tragedy of the Jews of Poland and Judaism worldwide. For a long time, the people of the entire world will remember the diabolical behavior of the Nazis. With the intent to whitewash that blackness, Germany arranges trials. The whole civilized world has also forgotten quickly: ironic courts and litigation, ironic settlements ... [But we] will not stop demanding, shouting, writing, talking."

What my father wrote so many years ago about those trials, and the sense of foreboding in his words, is quite relevant today: "They talk of punishments and once again in almost all the countries swastikas are appearing in the streets and on Jewish houses ... I let myself ask our God: How long? How much more?" Back then, he proclaimed openly the obligation of the Jews to defend themselves and not be deceived "by a smile," and to root out any Nazi or neo-Nazi threat before it had a chance to grow. I do not remember what my father said upon returning from Germany. I was 18 years old. He could have taken me with him. He did not suggest it, nor would I have gone. I strongly rejected Germany and the Germans. I was not afraid for my physical safety; but I was terrified by the images that the mere idea of Germany brought to my mind.

As time passed, many happy family events helped my parents heal and perhaps even recover their faith in life. In 1967 I married my life-long boyfriend, Rafael Gelman, and eventually we had three children, the first grandchildren in the family. My mother became a fantastic grandmother, totally devoted to the little ones, as was my father. Our children adored their grandparents. My mother saw them nearly every day, took them walking, told them stories. They often spent the weekend at my parents' house where my mother spoiled them and delighted in cooking their favorite dishes. When my siblings married the family again grew, with more grandchildren coming along. My parents were exceptionally proud of their children and their children's families. They would often travel to visit the ones who did not reside in Venezuela. Rafael and I stayed in Maracaibo, close to my parents.

My father was a strong and healthy man. As he aged, he would say: "I am afraid of being like my great-grandmother, Ita Leah, who lived to be 103." In 1991, when he was 87, he began deteriorating mentally and physically. After a lifetime of being dependent on her husband, my mother had to take on all the responsibilities and she began to make her own decisions, showing a strength we had never seen in her. Episodes of depression became less frequent, and she began to talk to her grandchildren about her history.

Rafael and I moved to Caracas in 1996 and my mother followed us. With great assurance, she bought an apartment in one day and chose to move at the same time we did. My parents – my mother especially – had become used to turning to me for help since I was the only one living near them. The move was the last act for which she sought assistance.

Caracas represented a rejuvenating change for her. The temperate climate delighted her, allowing her to enjoy nature to the full. She went walking in a park almost every morning. "Why do you not come? It is so pretty," she used to say. She was enamored of the scenery offered by the majestic Avila Mountains overlooking the city. She renewed old friendships, going out frequently, on her own or with us. Caracas' Jewish community was larger than that in Maracaibo and sponsored many kinds of activities – religious, cultural, and social. She wanted to take advantage of all of them. Now that she was arranging her own schedule and travels, my children would joke, "Mother, admit it, Grandma does not need you anymore."

In April 1996, she agreed to grant an interview about her Holocaust experiences to the USC Shoah Foundation: The Institute for Visual History and Education, which was established by Steven Spielberg in 1994. During the recorded conversation, she was able to speak calmly and openly about the event which had always tormented her: the element of luck that had been hers, allowing her to be saved in place of Esther. Whenever she got together with her friend and soul sister Sara Omelinski in Israel, the two of them would talk about how lucky they had been. During the war, they were together with Esther, and Sara's sisters and mother, but only she and Sara had survived. In remembering with Sara, she would always say: "We were really fortunate during the war, being together the whole time. Hil helped me, without him it would not have happened. I often think that if she [Esther] had not been sick when they started the roundup, she might have gotten away. She too made good decisions, but she had bad luck. It was like that in the war, impossible to guess." Sara survived because "when they were in Adampol she was accepted by Moshe Lichtenberg's partisan group, she also had luck there."

I listened to the interview only once and had a strange reaction. I avoided bringing up the subject with my mother. I was not ready to face my parents' history, to get truly close to their feelings. Because of his mental and physical state, I could not talk to my father. With my mother, I justified my silence by telling myself that I might only be reviving the depression she had suffered with for so long. So I buried my anxieties deep inside, not realizing that by the time of that interview she was ready to tell over and over her story and my father's. The deep sorrow she endured throughout her existence became such an integral part of who she was that she could now speak of the war without getting upset. When she got together with other survivors in Caracas, this was a common subject of conversation. They would share their stories and their sufferings. Joseph, our second son, eventually interviewed her at length and my brother, Leo, also went over much information with her – he also organized the only photos we have of my father's family. As for me, I never made up my mind to approach her to hear the details of her history.

At the end of the interview, my mother left us an important message in harmony with her ideas: "The first thing I wish to say to you is that you should not forget, that you should follow the traditions. Since our people are not great in number, we must try to stay united and help Israel to have a homeland. Those [Jewish people] who are abroad in the Diaspora do not realize the importance of this as much as someone who has suffered such a great tragedy. If Israel had existed back then, many people could have been saved, but it was not so, they had nowhere to go .... In our city, which had some 5,600 Jews, only 50 young people survived. My family had been living there for decades, my grandparents, great grandparents ... maybe 1,000 individuals, and not one was left."

In 1997, my father died in Caracas, at 92 years of age. We took his remains to Israel. My mother, who had cared for him with devotion, overcame her sadness surrounded by a family nucleus that gave her support. A few years later, in June of 2000, her first great-grandchild, a girl, was born. My mother, proud and happy, rejoiced with all of us. This birth was both a sign of our continuity and the reason for keeping our traditions and values alive.

14

RETURN TO POLAND

My mother and I, along with my sister, Rosa, and my brother, Leo, were among a group of 38 survivors and relatives who traveled to Poland in September of 2000. During the journey from Warsaw to Włodawa we stopped in various cities. Of her native land, my mother knew well only her own shtetl, where she had spent her childhood and some of her youth. Yet in every location we visited, I was aware of how she – grieving but alert – silently faced the disheartening scenes that came before her eyes: synagogues, cemeteries, little monuments, all essentially abandoned and deteriorating, the ruins of Polish Jewry. She looked everything over carefully, reading the occasional plaque, lost in thought. Only in Krakow did she make a comment, after listening to the stories about Schindler and other Poles who had risked their lives to help Jews: "I believe Jews had a better chance in the big cities than in the smaller towns. Maybe there were more Poles ready to help and more places to hide. I do not hold any resentment toward the Poles, it was hard for them. If they protected Jews and got caught, they could be killed too." As for me, I felt overwhelmed and saddened but was not sure why. I hoped that the coming days might shed more light on my emotional reactions to our trip.

During our lengthy journey, the survivors talked about their ordeals. There was a great solidarity, an outpouring of recollections. My mother knew few of these people prior to our trip, but quickly became part of the group. On hearing them relate how they had faced death every day, and had clung to life from moment to moment, I asked myself what trick of fate allowed them to overcome so much adversity and keep moving forward. I understood better the daily struggles of my mother and all the others, their stories coming together to form a common portrait of suffering and survival.

My mother, in turn, told of her own (and my father's) experiences with a surprising serenity that left no room for anguish. I tried to figure out why she decided to return, what impelled her to undertake this trip, not just to Włodawa but to the concentration camps and other sites in Poland. When I asked her why, she said: "After the war, we only thought about getting away from here. Never to see any of this again, never to return to Poland. Yet now I understand it was right to come, to see the camps, to verify that all was true and to realize again that I, myself, never came face to face with death. It was just luck and I never understood why."

While listening to her, I pictured her as a young girl surrounded by her father and her siblings, tied to them, depending on them, and admiring Esther especially. Because of the war she had to grow up fast. Under normal circumstances, she might have learned to be more decisive, more independent, but during those uncertain times she relied on others to make her decisions – her father, Esther, and my father. She had luck on her side as well, as many of the survivors did.

At the start of the trip, another traveler named Pnina Rubaka introduced herself to my mother. Pnina's father had owned a shop in the rynek, next to Grandfather Moses' grocery. Strangely, my mother did not remember her although they were around the same age. That may have been because Pnina's family was not religious, which meant the two girls moved in different circles. Once they got to know each other, Pnina and my mother spent much time together exchanging stories. Pnina also remembered my father with gratitude, for he had helped her set up a hideout before the fifth roundup. Thanks to him she had escaped. Others from the group approached us to talk about Hil Grunhaus. We were already aware that due to his generosity and readiness to assist anyone in need he was well known in Włodawa. It made us happy to know that survivors thought of him in this way. As Sara remarked: "Hil was kindhearted and generous with his resources – he could get whatever was needed."

On the way to Włodawa we passed through miles and miles of wooded areas, one after another. Pines, elms, beeches, then dense thickets of tall pines where little light entered. Forests, alternating with tiny villages and stretches of grassland. At last, we arrived. As we stepped off the bus, the first thing we encountered was a battery of television cameras filming "the Jews who were returning to their town." Many were interviewed, among them my mother and Sara. My mother was disoriented, confused. She realized we were in the rynek, the central square.

Rynek, Włodawa, September 2000

We looked for number 22 where her father's store had been, but we did not see it. The numbers had changed. All around the square stood rows of light-colored, nondescript buildings that housed small shops, structures erected during the communist era. The city had been somewhat modernized. There were phone booths, Coca-Cola signs, and decorated store fronts. A few wooden hovels were still standing. There were no Jews among the current 15,000 inhabitants. To my mother it appeared the town had changed and, very frustrated, she told us she did not like the place, it seemed ugly. Another survivor, a partisan who was searching for his house in the rynek, suggested we walk to the street behind to try to spot something they would recognize. My mother, annoyed, did not want to, although she finally went along. That did not make it any easier for her. "I have never been here before," she said, no longer interested in finding her father's store.

Suddenly, we heard someone calling her: "Sheindele, Sheindele!" It was a friend, Efraim Fishman, a partisan from Lichtenberg's group. He came up and gave her a big, loving hug. The two of them had met several times on trips to Israel and she was happy to see him again. They stood and chatted animatedly in Yiddish for a while. Finally, I saw her smile for the first time since we had arrived in Włodawa, her city.

We then headed for the Great Synagogue, which was right downtown. It was a complex of three buildings which had miraculously escaped destruction. It had been turned into a museum – the Muzeum Zespół Synagogalny we Włodawa. We entered and immediately found ourselves before the beautiful polychrome Aron HaKodesh (a cabinet holding holy books) that had been restored in 1936 and was still just as breathtaking. My mother found it quite lovely and gazed at it for quite some time. After that she carefully examined the photos of Jewish Włodawa, put on display in the hope that people might recognize someone they knew. Her father seemed to be in one of those pictures, but the image was not clear enough. Looking at the exhibit, her face lit up with pride as she repeated comments that we had heard her make so often: "Do you see that though it was small, Włodawa was a city with great community activity? All the Jewish organizations were functioning, both religious and secular, and the youth movements. There was solidarity and we helped the needy." Those photos took her back to her Włodawa, the one she continually talked about. They lightened her mood and let her forget for a while the disappointment she had experienced since arriving in her hometown.

Synagogue, Włodawa, September 2000

Aron Hakodesh, Włodawa, September 2000

Our hotel was in Okuninka, about eight kilometers from Włodawa. It overlooked a lake, one of seven in the area. Our first morning there, my mother woke me up to look out our window at the view, saying in astonishment: "I never realized there were lakes around here, I only knew our river, the Bug."

Sobibor, September 2000

We spent that morning visiting Sobibor. On the road, my mother gazed at the woods which to me did not seem very dense or very safe, but she disagreed and told us of the many Jews that had saved themselves by hiding among those trees. At Sobibor we walked around what was left of the camp, absorbed in our thoughts and our sorrow.[1] Standing solemnly in prayer under the Israeli flag, we lit candles in remembrance of our loved ones, then retraced our steps to stop at the little museum. My mother wanted her picture taken by the memorial plaque the group donated and before leaving she asked us to write in the visitors' book. Her entry read: "I am deeply sad because you are not here." She said to me: "Now do you understand why I am always sad?"

Włodawa Municipal Park, September 2000

On the way back to Włodawa my mother spoke once again about the deaths of her sister Deborah and Deborah's family, repeating a thought she had often expressed: "For me the worst was when they separated parents from their children, I do not think I could have gone on living after that. To abandon a child is the worst." All of us were drained, her especially. Back in the city, we sat down to rest and after a while she wanted to look for her school on Piłsudskiego Street. As she was not sure how far up the street it was and she did not have the energy to go too far, we only walked a couple of blocks and ended up at the city park. She sighed: "Do you see how pretty it is with all those leafy trees? We played here a lot."

Rosa and I wanted to see the places where our parents had lived. We found Wyrykowska Street, which is downtown. We went looking for number 46, the Grunhaus home, in vain. The numbers went up to 22 then started again at 10. The street extended, unpaved, through a deserted area full of rubble and garbage, and there were no house numbers. Later, we learned that all the dwellings on that street were demolished after the war, to be replaced by the small structures Rosa and I had seen. My mother had given us the Grunhaus address, but she did not remember her own; oddly enough she showed no interest in seeing her family home, perhaps because of the intense emotions she was experiencing on the trip. Now we know it was on Błotna Street, in downtown Włodawa, and that neither her house nor the dwellings that surrounded it are still standing.

We spent our last day in Włodawa. On the way to the Bug River, we visited a church. My mother had never been in it, but she asked Pnina, her old neighbor and now her confidante, whether she had ever been inside. Pnina said yes, and she proceeded to tell us the story. She said that one day a couple from another town came to get married there, and when the wedding party arrived in the city they honked the horns of their vehicles, so she and her friends followed them to the church and ended up going in to watch the ceremony. Then Pnina had another story that made my mother laugh. Whenever Pnina and her nonobservant friends saw some of my mother's religious male cousins walking down the street, the girls would stand side by side to keep them from getting by since the boys were not supposed to walk between two women. My mother listened to those anecdotes in amazement. She remarked that she and Pnina had grown up in the same shtetl but in completely different ways.

We went down to the Bug along Mostowa Street, the same route Jews had to take to the train station when they were sent to Sobibor. We passed by a mill in ruins, a place my mother recognized immediately: "This was the house of a wealthy family. They had a young son I gave lessons to during the first year of the war. He came to my house, and I taught him to read and write. I never knew what happened to him." At the Bug we saw a narrow stream, its water greenish, its banks covered with thick, unkempt vegetation. Not a pretty site at all, I thought. But I did not dare share that impression with my mother. For her, the Bug was wider and swifter and the river was part of her most precious recollections. She repeated nostalgically things we already knew: the springtime excursions to pick berries in the fields, the strolls to the riverbank, the Saturday walks with her girlfriends, the afternoons with her maternal grandmother, the winter cold with the Bug frozen over, the sledding. All those stories brought back her childhood and youth, the happiest period of her life.

As my mother talked, again my mind went back in time and I tried to picture her at school, at home, on the banks of the Bug during vacations, and with her younger siblings and then, during the war, enduring hunger and cold, fighting fear and misery as she lost those she loved, one by one.

Unexpectedly, a woman approached my mother and Pnina. The three of them had a long, lively conversation in Polish and then said goodbye with hugs and kisses. My mother explained that this Polish lady was the daughter of a Jew who was married to a Christian woman from Włodawa, who had saved her husband during the war by hiding him. When the daughter found out a group of Jewish survivors was in town, she came out to meet some of them. My mother said that she would have been interested in hearing about more such cases of Jews who had been hidden and saved.

The daughters of a survivor who had been a policeman during the war were on the trip with us. Since the father was in ill health, he had sent his children instead. The two women kept somewhat apart from the group, and it upset my mother that some of the people did not want to associate with them. My mother had known the father and assured us he was a good person who found himself obliged to join the Jewish police.

That afternoon we headed for Adampol, passing by longer stretches of forest than we had seen previously. We stopped at a farm and spoke with a family who remembered the exact date of the last roundup at Adampol: August 13, 1943. They told us how the Germans had arrived early and murdered all the Jews there. My mother asked Sara to go look for the plaque commemorating the event. She knew this probably was not the spot where Esther had died, yet she had her picture taken there. For her, the pilgrimage to the place where her sister had lost her life was one of the most significant and sorrowful moments of the trip.

Back on the bus, she seemed perturbed. She had always wanted to return to Adampol with Sara so they could put up a memorial plaque for Esther, regardless of not knowing exactly where it should go. Her thoughts were going back to the moment she and Esther had to say goodbye and her heart was reliving the grief caused by Esther's death. As we were driving through a forest on a long straight road, she told us softly: "I left with the partisans on a road similar to this one, and when we were at the crossroads, I glanced back, and I could see Esther standing there, still looking at me. Sara found out from her sisters, and told me much later, that Esther had spent the whole night crying."

When we got back to Włodawa my mother wanted to try to locate her school again. We had to leave so there was no time. I imagine she was trying to recapture the Włodawa of her past, a place that no longer existed. I saw how hard it was for her to say goodbye to the religious, ultraconservative world of her youth, even though it had already disappeared. My sister and brother and I, on the other hand, only wanted to get away. If it had not been for our mother, we never would have visited Włodawa. It was her desire to undertake the trip that motivated me to accompany her, no other reason. A deep sense of loss overcame me and, although at that moment I was not capable of perceiving it, the trip helped me face my ghosts. The gray shadow that had been my companion all my life now acquired substance. It represented the Jewish Włodawa in ruins, with an aura of suffering: war, fear, roundups, cold and hunger, Sobibor, extermination, a daily struggle for survival ... Maybe in the depths of my soul I was searching for a world I had imagined and wanted to find; but like my mother, reality had made me feel like an outsider, alien to the people and places of Włodawa.

During the trip I thought a lot about my father, who had never gone back to Poland. He used to say there was nothing left there, not even his family's graves. In my eyes he was a strong figure, circumspect, closed in on himself. The one time I saw him cry, I almost went into shock. We were in Jerusalem planting a little grove of trees in honor of our loved ones killed in the Shoah. When he began reciting the El

Malei Rachamim, the prayer for the deceased, he burst out sobbing and could not stop. All the grief he had kept inside for so long came to the surface and poured out as he was praying.

For me each day of our trip was filled with memorable moments, difficult but extraordinary. I finally understood why my mother had decided to return to Poland: To say a final goodbye, to comprehend that her family and her world had disappeared, and to confirm that her tormenting memories were just that, memories. Perhaps being accompanied by us, her children, helped her realize life had triumphed over the kingdom of evil. Our presence affirmed that her struggles had not been in vain. Regardless of their efforts, the Nazis had not succeeded in exterminating her people.

The trip ended and we all flew to our various destinations. My mother went back to Israel with my brother Leo, to enjoy some time with her son and his family. Three days later, she was in the hospital, and I arrived to be at her bedside. The week she lay ill she was serene and talkative, relating new stories as she seemed to have found an inner peace she had not enjoyed for years. "Now all I want to talk about is the war and Poland," were her words. Perhaps that journey to the past had helped her close a chapter. She was beginning another stage of her existence, happier and freer from her suffering than she had ever been, moving from being a victim to being a survivor. Her depression was born in Poland and 55 years later, also in Poland, it was buried for good. In the hospital, her condition worsened. She underwent surgery but it was too much for her heart. On September 29, 2000, an hour before Rosh Hashanah – and just ten days after returning from Poland – my mother died in Tel Aviv. With her sudden passing, one of her greatest wishes was granted: to die in Israel and be buried there. A few days before leaving on the Poland trip, she had expressed this desire to one of her grandchildren, not imagining how soon it would be fulfilled. Now she rests there next to my father in the land they both loved dearly, and that contributed so greatly to the recovery of their faith in life.

*The plaque SCENE OF NAZI CRIMES 1939-1944, Adampol,
September 2000*

APPENDICES

Bernhard Falkenberg, Righteous Among the Nations

Bernhard Falkenberg was born on November 22, 1902, in Flatow, Germany, the son of farmers.

His father died when Bernhard was 13, leaving him to help his mother work the land. In 1927, he went out on his own and took a job as a soil analyst. He was involved in politics from an early age, first as a member of the Democratic Socialist Party (SPD), later joining the Communist Party (KPD). After a brief stay in jail for distributing communist propaganda in Flatow, he turned to working as a foreman for soil analysis firms in Berlin. At the same time, he was studying to be a civil engineer.

Falkenberg arrived in Włodawa on September 10, 1940, when the war was well underway. He came as an employee of a German, Wilhem Rohde, who had several ongoing projects in the city. When Rohde returned to Germany, Falkenberg, who had worked with him in Berlin since 1938, took on several responsibilities under the orders of Franz Holtzheimer. From the beginning, his decisive intervention on behalf of the Jews was in many ways exceptional. It began by hiring many more workers than necessary since people with jobs received extra food rations. He also used his position to obtain information on roundups and other actions so he could warn Jews, allowing many of them to take refuge and hide on his property. Because Falkenberg remained on good terms with the Germans, after Włodawa was declared Judenrein, he went on working there with Polish employees and stayed in touch with the Jewish partisans, to whom he supplied food, money, and blankets.

In July 1943, Moshe Lichtenberg, one of the partisan leaders in the Włodawa area, wrote Falkenberg a note to be delivered by a Pole from Adampol. The man was detained and beaten until he confessed and handed over the message. The same day, a member of the Gendarmerie, Josef Schmidt, went to Falkenberg's house and told him what had happened. When the policeman found a pistol on the bed, he arrested Falkenberg and took him to the police station. He was charged for collaborating with the partisans since the note was a request for 5,000 złotys and food supplies. On July 20, he was transferred to Chelm and turned over to the Gestapo. A statement from Willy Selinger, the German in charge of Adampol, accused him of having been seen frequently in the woods with Jews, giving them food and killing a deer to provide them with meat. The Germans reproached him for his connections with Jewish partisans. Despite all these allegations he was never mistreated. In December, he was taken to Kazimierz along with 15 Poles who were soon murdered. Only Falkenberg was spared. They interrogated him again and made him sign a confession. Sent first to Lublin, then to Warsaw, Poznań, and Vienna, on December 17, 1943, he was interned at the Mauthausen concentration camp in Austria. He was liberated on May 6, 1945, when the Americans arrived at the camp. Falkenberg's wife, Emma, was imprisoned in Berlin for 11 months, then released following a statement by Gendarmerie Lieutenant Luitpold Fuhrmann which exonerated her.

The same year Falkenberg returned to what in 1949 would become East Germany and decided to settle north of Berlin, in Mehrow, a town in the Ahrensfelde municipality. Over the next four years his main occupation was the farming of some land he bought there. On

June 5, 1946, the magistrate of Berlin officially recognized Falkenberg as a "victim of fascism." Still a communist at heart, he joined the Democratic Farmers' Party and served as the mayor of Mehrow from 1949 to 1950. The term ended upon his arrest for smuggling to West Germany the sugar beet juice produced on his property. The authorities took away his pension and his status as a victim of fascism. It seems he never spoke of his past, so few knew of his brave actions to save Jewish lives. After being released, he worked in an agricultural cooperative until 1961. On April 29, 1962, he took part in the inquiries carried out in Bernau for the dossier against Nitschke and his associates, which was being prepared in Hanover. On July 20, he testified in Hanover at the same time as Franz Holtzheimer.

Grete Rotstein, one of the 50 women who took refuge in Falkenberg's house during the final Włodawa roundup, was living in Israel yet never forgot the man who had helped her. In 1961, she heard about the case being prepared against Nitschke and his associates and she found out Falkenberg was alive. She did not stop until she found him and wrote to him. In his reply, Falkenberg told her about his arrest and his imprisonment at Mauthausen, expressing his happiness at receiving news of people he had protected during that terrible war.

In 1964 when they were in Hanover for the trial, Falkenberg and Holtzheimer met and went to the courthouse together. Entering the building, Falkenberg ran into defendant Josef Schmidt, the officer who had arrested him in Włodawa in 1943. He gave Schmidt a scornful look, saying, "I am proud and happy to be able to walk with my head held high."

Many of the Jewish survivors were also there in Hanover. It must have been an emotional encounter, with Falkenberg no doubt telling of his days in prison and his economic and legal difficulties. Thanks to sworn statements on his behalf provided by my father, and Franz Holtzheimer – and because of his own testimony at the trial – Falkenberg was officially vindicated. They reinstated his pension, returning the identity document which recognized him as a victim of fascism. On July 16, 1965, he once again testified in the Bernau

Regional Court. There the lawyers questioned him on other matters, such as what he knew about the Sobibor camp, the conduct of Dr. Werner Ansel (head of the Chelm Security Police), and the fate of the Vienna Jews who came to Włodawa.

Bernhard Falkenberg died in Berlin on June 24, 1966. Later, in October 1969, thanks to the efforts of Włodawa survivors, he was recognized as "Righteous Among the Nations" by Yad Vashem.[1] A tree in his honor was planted in the Garden of the Righteous and his name appears on the Wall of Honor, distinguished with the number four.

When a reporter asked Grete what she thought compelled Falkenberg to take the risk of helping Jews, she answered categorically: "Falkenberg was a decent human being. And it is interesting that he was a quiet and wise man. He was – and I think that he is still like that today – a humble man. He helped everyone he could help. Without distinction. When I remember those days, it seems to me that he concerned himself all the time only with saving Jews. I never dared ask him [...] why he really helped us. For me he was the epitome of a man, the epitome of a "Righteous Among the Nations."[2]

There is no doubt that the figure of Falkenberg occupies a special place in the history of the Jews of Włodawa. On his own he became involved in the terrible tragedies unfolding before his eyes, saving as many as possible without asking anything in return. He belonged to a heroic group of human beings who acted according to their convictions, knowing full well they were risking their own lives.

The Hanover Trial

On November 24, 1960, at the request of the Włodawa survivors, Yad Vashem contacted the Zentrale Stelle der Landesjustizverwaltungen (also known as the Z Commission) in Ludwigsburg, Germany – the body created to prosecute those accused of Nazi war crimes – and asked that Richard Nitschke be found. After the war, Nitschke lived in

Germany under the name Neumann. In 1954 – the year he rejoined his wife, who was living in Sievershausen – he began to once again use his real name. In 1960, the couple moved to Hanover. On February 15, 1961, Prosecutor Gerhard Ilhe requested an arrest warrant be issued for Nitschke. He was apprehended on May 4, and on May 8 he was subjected to an interrogation.

At the same time, the prosecutor began to gather further information, using the contacts of the Jewish World Congress and Yad Vashem, and to draw up lists of possible witnesses. Upon being questioned, potential witnesses were asked to explain the events that occurred in Włodawa from November 1939 until July 1943 and describe to the greatest detail possible the roles played by Nitschke and the other accused men. On July 24, 1963, Ilhe produced a 57-page report, which enabled him to support an indictment. However, since some of the assertions would have been hard to verify because the witnesses had not personally been present during certain incidents, the prosecutor was obliged to drop some of charges.

The trial took place in 1964 in the Hanover Regional Court (Landgericht Hannover) between May 11 and October 29. It began with a summary of the indictment and the presentation of the life histories of all the accused. Next came the witness statements and the questioning of witnesses and defendants.

The principal defendant, Richard Nitschke (born on March 22, 1898), had arrived in Włodawa in November 1939. He was coming from a career in counterespionage. As a second lieutenant stormtrooper in the SS, he headed the Włodawa border control post from November 1939 until the end of 1942. The Border Police were attached to the Gestapo (or Secret State Police) and handled all matters having to do with Jews. In January 1943, Nitschke left Włodawa to become the chief of the SS in Kazimierz Dolny. He was indicted for his part in 25 criminal acts committed in the two towns where he had served.

Hubert Schönborn, first sergeant and sergeant major in the SS, was also arrested in 1961. Questioned during the preliminary investigation, he was charged with six criminal acts. He committed suicide in jail in early May 1964, at the start of the trial.

Anton Müller, sergeant major in the SS Border Police, was arrested December 1, 1961, and was accused of taking part in 18 criminal acts.

Adolf Schaub, detained May 3, 1962, had started out as Nitschke's interpreter and in 1940 and 1941 served with the Border Police. He was charged on six counts.

Luitpold Fuhrmann, head of the Włodawa Gendarmerie was accused of two crimes.

Josef Schmidt, briefly in charge of the Włodawa Gendarmerie, was indicted for his part in four criminal acts.

The case proceeded in the following manner: the bulk of the testimony had been collected in preliminary statements made by witnesses before the trial. Then, during the trial the witness would answer some specific questions, with the defendants given the opportunity to formulate a comment on what had been declared. More than 100 witnesses were asked about the five Włodawa roundups, the object being to discern what person or persons had been in charge, who had played a role, and who had carried out murders. The prosecutor, convinced of the guilt of all the accused, Nitschke especially, focused on two aspects of the crimes: on the one hand, the responsibility of each defendant based on his individual criminal acts, and on the other, the collective responsibility for helping send 7,000 victims to extermination at Sobibor.

Ilhe wanted the maximum penalty for Nitschke but without a confession or eyewitness accounts of the killings, his hands were tied. Accordingly, he started the trial with Nitschke as the main defendant, hoping to find more substantial evidence over the course of the questioning. Nitschke had been subjected to several medical tests prior to the trial and because the doctors certified he was fit enough to appear in court and testify, the proceedings got underway. On May 12, the physician from the prosecutor's office examined him and determined he could only be on the stand three to four hours a day.

Bernhard Falkenberg and many of the survivors testified that on numerous occasions Nitschke himself committed murders or ordered others to do so. In his statement Falkenberg pointed out: "I know quite well that both Nitschke and other members of the SD and the Gendarmerie were aware that people were sent to Sobibor to be exterminated. That they did not know is untrue; every little child in Włodawa could smell the Sobibor chimneys." He accused Nitschke of having personally directed the second and third roundups. For his part, Nitschke tried to deny his responsibility. When questioned about his part in the third roundup he admitted to being there, claiming that one of the heads of the Lublin SS had been in charge and his own role had been limited to "giving orders to his subordinates." All the witnesses, however, offered detailed descriptions of Nitschke's supervision of the event. The other four accused men admitted taking part but tried to minimize their offenses by putting the blame on the troops brought in as reinforcements during the roundup.

Over the course of the questioning, it was obvious that the defendants' excuse for the crimes committed was "obedience to the rules." The major argument used to justify their acts was that they were "carrying out orders" and that they could not or would not have dared to disobey. From one moment to the next they recognized that those orders had a criminal end – the systematic, large-scale slaughter of Jews. Their actions contradicted what they were alleging in their defense. Just by complying with those orders, they committed countless crimes. Müller was the only one who seemed to repent momentarily: "During that era, I did not have the courage to resist. I feel deeply for the victims." For his part, Nitschke emphasized that all his men, without exception, obeyed his orders and never objected.

The German press followed the trials closely, with the public showing little interest. It was the period of the Frankfurt and Düsseldorf trials of the Auschwitz, Treblinka, and Majdanek perpetrators. Those events attracted more attention. And even though the Hanover prosecutor tried to show that low-ranking officials had also committed individual and collective murders, there were few spectators during the deliberations. In an article published in *Die Welt* on August 12, 1964, the reporter describes Nitschke's appearance: "This is the portrait of a nervous man who stammers and speaks with difficulty. Partially paralyzed, it is hard for him to speak or walk, and he bursts into tears readily." After summarizing some of the Włodawa roundups, the journalist points out how Nitschke, despite the testimony heard, persists in his lies, continuing to repeat his assertions: "I did not realize Sobibor was an extermination camp. I thought it was a secret laboratory for weapons testing. If I had known back then what I know now, I would rather they had killed me. Never in my life did I execute a defenseless person. I only shot partisans or ordered someone else to do so."

Nitschke testified almost every day and the length of the sessions depended on his physical condition. There were frequent interruptions when he would claim to be ill and could not follow the accusations right then. After being examined at the hospital in Hanover on August 19, the conclusion was that he could testify. By September 18, the prosecutor had obtained enough evidence to accuse Nitschke of murder in four cases and of playing a role in the collective slaughter of more than 7,000 persons. Ilhe stated: "Nitschke became a criminal through cowardice. He lost all moderation. Since he had been a baker's helper, once they let him put on the trappings of an official, he was ready and willing to show his gratitude. This is the only explanation that lets us understand how [Nitschke] ordered murders and committed them himself." The prosecutor sought life imprisonment for Nitschke. Though he acknowledged the defendant was obeying orders, he also took into consideration that there had not been the slightest sign of repentance for the crimes committed. October 12 was the last day Nitschke appeared in court. The following day he was admitted to the hospital in Hanover. The doctors doubted he could continue to testify, so they consulted with a neurologist who decided he could indeed, but not for the time being. In view of the situation, on October 19, the prosecutor decided to separate Nitschke's trial from that of the other four so that they could proceed. All the witnesses had spoken and now it was the turn of the defense.

On October 13, the reporter covering the case for *Die Welt,* and looking ahead to the verdict, wrote: "What makes this trial so extraordinary is that never before has it been made so clear how 'ordinary people' are capable of closing their minds to the murderous acts of Hitler, even in the face of obligatory orders." The prosecutor did not consider the "following of orders" to be a valid excuse for any of the five defendants. As a result, if Nitschke's involvement had been under examination, the sentence would have been quite severe. Ilhe's thinking about Müller and Schaub was along the same lines: they could have refused to take part in the roundups; they chose to do the contrary. For Müller who admitted killing nine people in Włodawa, the prosecutor sought 12 years in prison, and eight years for Schaub.

Nevertheless, when the jury's verdict was announced on October 29, 1964 (and confirmed by the Superior Court on July 12, 1965) the sentences proved lenient and were denounced in the press. The court determined that "the extermination of the Jewish people was murder" and of the deportation of more than 7,000 people to the concentration camp at Sobibor, it deemed that "the memory of the witnesses was not that accurate," which prevented clearly establishing who was guilty. The text of each sentence reads like an apology by the court.

All the defendants were deprived of their civil rights. The sentences are as follows:

Müller: Five years, for complicity in six instances of homicide. Years spent in preventive detention since December 1, 1961, counted as time served.

Shaub: Two years and three months, for complicity in two cases of homicide. Sentence fulfilled by time in prison from May 3, 1962, while awaiting trial.

Fuhrmann: Two years for complicity in two homicides. Time spent incarcerated in Lublin until 1950 counted so he did not have to go to prison.

Schmidt: Two years and six months for homicide in two instances. Required to serve full sentence.

Meanwhile, Nitschke's health continued to deteriorate. Exams performed on October 22, 1965, and January 18, 1966, refer to heart problems and dementia. As a result, on January 30, 1966, he was declared unfit to stand trial and further proceedings were postponed. Nitschke died that same year.

Throughout the trial there was an atmosphere of great tension. From the outset, Prosecutor Ilhe, convinced of the defendants' guilt, had sought imprisonment for Nitschke and significant penalties for the other four. The defense disagreed and the court clearly went along with that, given the token sentences it handed down. The press, on the other hand, denounced from the start the intent to banalize the Włodawa events. They were not happy with the verdict. Although it "was a question of low-ranking officials who were obeying orders," compliance with those orders meant they had committed countless murders and had participated in the extermination of 7,000 Jews. Those men deserved sentences in accordance with the gravity of their actions. Without a doubt, those ridiculous verdicts gave in to the policy then prevalent in Germany: to minimize and forget the crimes of the past.

ACKNOWLEDGMENTS

In writing my parents' story, the collaboration of many individuals and institutions was of vital importance. First, special thanks to Mihaela Metianu, Executive Director of the Center for Global Engagement at Florida Atlantic University, who granted me the time needed to carry out this project.

At FAU I had the unconditional support of Dr. Alan Berger, Raddock Family Eminent Scholar Chair for Holocaust Studies, whose classes allowed me to expand my knowledge of the Holocaust.

At Yad Vashem I must mention many: Dr. David Silberklang, senior historian, and former director of the journal *Yad Vashem Studies,* who kindly advised me throughout my research; Perla Hazán, who was of great help in leading me to contacts at the institution; Irena Steinfeldt, from the Department of the Righteous Among the Nations; and Fani Molad, Shaul Ferrero, and Timorah Perel, who obtained the testimony of the Włodawa survivors and material on the Hanover trial from the archives.

At the United States Holocaust Memorial Museum (USHMM), help from Vincent Slatt, Steven Vitto, and Megan Lewis enabled me to establish precise dates and places for my parents' journey, and Peter Black provided me with information on the final verdict in the Hanover trial. To all of them, my appreciation.

In searching for my family in civil registries I had much assistance from Robinn Magid, Assistant Director of JRI-Poland (Jewish Records Indexing-Poland), and the help of Tadeusz Przystojecki in collecting further information about my ancestry.

I also offer thanks to the staff at Niedersächsisches Landesarchiv Hauptstaatsarchiv (Lower Saxony State Archives) in Hanover for granting me access to its archives.

To complete the material on my parents' story, I had recourse to several valuable interviews and statements from family and friends. Special recognition goes to Sara Omelinski, my mother's great friend who lovingly agreed to answer my questions, regardless of how hard it must have been for her to remember those times.

My niece Liran Grunhaus led me to Peter Kamber whose dedicated collaboration was of inestimable value, both for research on Bernhard Falkenberg and on the Hanover trial. Kamber unselfishly provided me all the material he had compiled on Falkenberg. His interest in the proceedings was such that of his own volition he traveled to Hanover and Ludwigsburg and searched the archives of the Z Commission to select information on the matter.

My deepest gratitude to my family for their unwavering affection and encouragement during all those years. To my husband, Rafael Gelman, for enduring with love and patience the endless days and nights of work. To my son Eli and my daughter Vanessa, for constantly cheering me on to complete my project, and to my son Joseph, for reading the first draft with great interest and being with me during the lengthy revision process. His keen observations contributed greatly to the final outcome. To my sister Rosa, for sharing with me memories that were essential for writing these pages, and to my brother Leo, for his never-ending interest in this story which belongs to all three of us alike. For the English version, I must especially mention and thank my sister Rosa, whose participation was decisive in this endeavor. And to my beloved grandchildren, some of whom have written pieces about their great-grandparents and are all excited over the prospect of having more detailed documentation of their family history.

My profound gratitude to the team accompanying me on the path to publication: Jenny Bemergui for her creative talent in design; Priscilla Abecasis, whose commitment and sensitivity gave the project a decisive orientation; and, above all, to Ana Caufman for sharing the passion for this story every step of the way.

My sincere thanks to my group of translators: Pamela Russ, who translated the material from *The Yizkor Book of Włodawa*; Luila Molina de Díaz, who did the translations from German; and Wiktoria Dines-Hubschmann, who translated the letters of my mother and Esther from Polish. For this English language version, I am grateful to Julia Shirek Smith, who worked long and hard to translate my parents' story in its entirety.

GLOSSARY

Aktzia: Polish term referring to the operation of rounding up Jews and sending them to extermination camps.

Aliyah: Immigration to Israel. In Hebrew the word means "ascent." Every Jew who returns to Israel is said to be making aliyah.

Beit Hamidrash: A center for religious studies.

Beit Yaakov: An education system for Jewish girls, founded by Sarah Schenirer in Poland in 1917. The schools were initially sponsored and subsidized by the local Agudat Yisrael and then became part of the Keren ha-Torah of the World Agudat Yisrael.

Brit Milah: The rite of circumcision performed on male Jews the eighth day after birth.

Endek: A member of the fascist antisemitic National Democratic Party (ND) of Poland.

Etrog and **Lulav:** A variety of bitter lemon (etrog) used with a bouquet of palm fronds and willow and myrtle boughs (lulav) for special blessings during Sukkoth.

Gabete: The woman in charge of maintaining order in the women's section of the synagogue, generally someone well versed in the prayers and rituals.

Gestapo: The secret state police of Nazi Germany.

Hanukkah: The Festival of Lights commemorating the recovery of Jerusalem and the rededication of the Second Temple in the Hellenic period, second century BC.

Hasidim: Followers of the ultra-Orthodox Hasidic Movement.

Hasidism: Popular religious movement (the Hasidic Movement) founded in the 18th century, propounding an Orthodox and mystical religious interpretation of Judaism.

Heder: Elementary Jewish school. plural is Heredim.

Joint (also known as the **JDC**): The American Jewish Joint Distribution Committee, founded in 1914. It is a North American Jewish aid organization headquartered in New York City.

Judenrein: Cleansed of Jews. A term used by the Nazis to refer to a city or shtetl from which they had removed all Jews.

Judenstadt: A city for Jews.

Judenwohnbezirk: Jewish residential zone in a city or shtetl.

Kehilla: The Jewish community in a country or a city. In the past, it was the body governing community life.

Kennkarte: Identity document issued by the German authorities in occupied countries during the Second World War. It was not given to Jews.

Kibbutz: A collective farm in Israel that is devoted to agriculture.

Kippah: A ritual cap worn by Jewish males.

Kosher: Food approved for consumption according to Jewish dietary laws.

Lager: A forced-labor camp.

Lebensraum: "German living space." Nazi Germany's belief that its borders should be expanded.

Matzo: An unleavened bread eaten during Passover.

Melamed (plural: Melamdim): Teacher in a Heder school.

Mikvah: Ritual bath.

Passover: Festival commemorating the exodus of the Jewish people from Egypt. For eight days only unleavened bread (matzos) is eaten.

Payot: Sideburns worn by Jewish men, resembling corkscrew curls.

Purim: Festival commemorating the Jews escape from massacre by the Persians.

Rosh Hashanah: The Jewish New Year.

Rynek: Main square or market square in a city, town, or village.

SA (Sturmabteilung): Nazi paramilitary organization.

Schutzpolizei: The uniformed police force (State protection police) of Nazi Germany.

SD (Sicherheitsdienst): Security Service of the SS.

Seder (Seudah): "Food served," the meal offered after a ceremony or on the morning and afternoon of Shabbat, following the religious service.

Shabbat: The seventh day after creation. It begins on Friday when the sun goes down. A day of rest, requiring compliance with certain established rules.

Shavuot: Festival to celebrate the handing of the Ten Commandments (Torah) to the Jewish people.

Shoah: Hebrew word for the Holocaust.

Shtetl: Name given to small towns in Eastern and Central Europe largely inhabited by Yiddish-speaking Jews.

Shtiebelej (or **Shtiebel**): Private houses of prayer.

SiPo (Sicherheitspolizei): German security police force created by Heinrich Himmler, SS leader and Chief of German Police, in 1936.

SS (Schutzstaffel): Combat unit of Nazi Germany which, under the orders of Heinrich Himmler, was tasked with implementing the Final Solution.

Sukkoth: Festival of the Booths, commemorating the stay of the Jews in the desert where they lived in tents exposed to the elements.

Szmalcownik: Individual dedicated to recognizing Jews and blackmailing them or turning them over to the Germans for a reward. Mostly active in cities.

Tallit: A kind of shawl worn by men during religious services.

Talmud Torah: Traditional Jewish community schools for the upper grades.

Torah: Text containing Jewish law. The Torah is made up of the first five books of the Old Testament, also known as the Pentateuch.

Tzitzit: Knotted fringes hanging from the ends of the tallit. They may also be found on an undergarment typically worn under a shirt by religious males.

Volksdeutsche: Persons of German origin living in different parts of Europe under other citizenship.

Yeshiva: A secondary school for rabbinical studies, historically open only to males.

Yizkor Books: Memory books, written and published by the Jewish survivors of a town or city.

Z Commission (Zentrale Stelle der Landesjustizverwaltungen): Main German agency created to prosecute those accused of Nazi war crimes.

Żydówka: Polish term for "Jewish girl," that was sometimes used in a derogatory way.

NOTES

2. Włodawa through the Ages

1. *Shtetl:* Small cities in central and eastern Europe with a majority population of Yiddish-speaking Jews.
2. For ease of reading, I shall refer to my parents by the names they adopted after the war, Hil Grunhaus Beckerman, and Alexandra Lederman Beckerman. For my closest relatives, I will use the names my parents used when speaking of them but will supply their given names (whatever part is known) in parentheses. For all others mentioned, I will quote their names as they appear in the Polish civil registries.

4. The Lederman Family

1. This revisionist Zionist organization, whose principal leader was Ze'ev Jabotinsky, grew rapidly in Poland before the war. Its two major objectives were to encourage emigration to Palestine and to create a Jewish state on both sides of the Jordan River.

5. The Bug River, Silent Witness

1. My mother's birth certificate states that she was born on December 21, 1922, not in 1924 as she said and certified on all later documents. The birth certificate was drawn up in 1930 from a declaration by her father, Moses. Did he or the notary make a mistake? By family lore, she was born on the first night of Hanukkah. Checking the Jewish calendar for 1922, we see that December 21 did not coincide with the first night of Hanukkah. The first night of Hanukkah in 1924 did occur on December 21, which would confirm my mother's birth year as 1924.

6. A Cosmopolitan Jew

1. My father's quotes come from the sources listed in the bibliography.
2. The *Yizkor Books* or *Memorial Books* are collections of texts written by the survivors of many communities in Europe to honor the memory of those who died in their shtetls or cities during the Holocaust. These works contain articles of various kinds: history, descriptions of cities, events of the war. The *Yizkor Book for Włodawa and the Sobibor Area*, specifically, includes contributions in Yiddish, Hebrew, and English.

3. Shimon Kanc, ed. *Yizkor Book for Włodawa and the Sobibor Area* (Tel Aviv: Włodawa Immigrants Association in Israel, 1974), pp. 315, 335.
4. Zishe Fuchs, "The First Aliyah," in *Yizkor Book for Włodawa*, pp. 383–385.

7. Life Disrupted

1. *Volksdeutsche:* Persons of German origin living in different parts of Europe under other citizenship.
2. *Sobibor* was one of the death camps built in Poland during the Second World War. Located about 11 kilometers southeast of Włodawa on the Chelm-Włodawa rail line, it was part of Operation Reinhardt (along with Belzec and Treblinka), which had been set up to exterminate the 2,284,000 Jews living in the General Government. The camp began operating in May 1942 and was shut down after an uprising that occurred on October 14, 1943. It is estimated that 180,000 died in this camp. Because of its strategic location close to this site and to rail lines, Włodawa served as a point where Jews were concentrated before being sent to Sobibor.
3. Incident mentioned in Ben-Zwia Holzmann, "The Tombstone Street," in *Yizkor Book for Włodawa*, pp. 49–52.

9. Fear, Death, and Destruction (Alexandra's Story)

1. The Oneg Shabbat Archives are a collection of clandestine documents compiled in the Warsaw Ghetto under the direction of the historian Emanuel Ringelblum. Many people worked to gather this information, to leave testimony on the lives of Jews in the ghetto and in all of Poland. The material was buried before the destruction of the ghetto. After the war only two containers of archives were found. The originals are stored at the Jewish Historical Institute in Warsaw.
2. Saul Friedländer, El *Tercer Reich y los judíos (1939–1945): Los años del exterminio.* Barcelona, Círculo de Lectores, S. A., 2009, p. 526
3. Sara Omelinski, "Great Action." In the *Yizkor Book*, pp. 67–68.
4. The *askaris* (also called "blacks" because of the color of their uniforms) were soldiers of various nationalities – Ukrainians, Latvians, Lithuanians – serving as volunteers in the German ranks. They were trained at the Trawniki SS camp for three basic functions: serving as concentration camp guards, helping with roundups, and carrying out mass executions.
5. Adampol, about seven kilometers from Włodawa was one of the subcamps set up in the area on Count Zamoyski's estate, which the Germans had confiscated. Many Jewish and Polish prisoners farmed the land or worked on water management for the area. In 1943, Willy Selinger became the camp director. He was an SS officer who liked to dress as a civilian. People have offered conflicting versions of his behavior. Some survivors said he was cruel to the Jews and mentioned that, without showing it overtly, he went along with the Germans' organizing of roundups in the place; others affirmed they had seen him murdering Jews; and finally, there were a few cases of people testifying that

Selinger had aided them. He was, however, called as a witness in the 1964 trial of Nitschke and his deputies. Selinger's evidence was shockingly superficial. He claimed ignorance of dates, names, culprits, not mentioning the date of the last roundup carried out in Adampol and Natalin. He did talk of murdered Jews. Supposedly, by that time he had been placed under house arrest and did not see anything.

10. The Survival Instinct (Hil's Story)

1. Episode reported by Grete Rotstein, Włodawa survivor, in Joseph Algazi's "The Story of a Communist 'Schindler'," *Shraga*-Elam (blog), *Blogspot,* September 20, 2010, http://shraga-elam.blogspot.com/ (Translated from Hebrew by George Malent).
2. Bernard Falkenberg, Testimony before the District Tribunal of Bernau, German Democratic Republic, July 16, 1965.
3. Hil Grunhaus, "Days and Years of Pain and Destruction," in *Yizkor Book,* pp. 568–602.
4. Falkenberg, Testimony.
5. Falkenberg, Testimony.
6. All the Aktzias started on the Shabbat or during Jewish holidays. Obviously, the Germans planned on demonstrating cruelty toward Jews at every moment.
7. Joseph Algazi, *The Story of a Communist Schindler.*

13. Venezuela: A New Life

1. Official Israeli institution created in Jerusalem in 1953 to preserve the memory of Holocaust victims.
2. Hil Grunhaus. Statement sworn before notary Erich Müller, Hanover, Germany, July 24, 1964.
3. Grunhaus, Statement sworn before notary. More on Falkenberg's detainment is provided in the Appendices.

14. Return to Poland

1. After our visit, Sobibor was closed for several years and reopened in 2019. It was rebuilt, preserving significant archeological discoveries: gas chambers and valuable objects that had belonged to victims who perished there.

Appendices

1. "Righteous Among the Nations" is a distinction conferred by the official Israel institution/museum Yad Vashem on non-Jews who risked their lives to save Jews during the Holocaust. The name comes from a phrase by Maimonides: "The

righteous of the nations of the world shall have a place in eternal life" (*Hiljot Melajim*, 8:11).

2. Algazi, *Communist Schindler*.

SOURCES

Algazi, Joseph. "The Story of a Communist 'Schindler'," *Shraga-Elam* (blog), *Blogspot,* September 20, 2010, http://shraga-elam. blogspot.com/(Translated from Hebrew by George Malent.)

Friedlander, Saul. *Nazi Germany and the Jews, 1939–1945: The Years of Extermination.* Vol. 2. New York: Harper Perennial, 2008.

Gilbert, Martin. *Holocaust Journey: Travelling in Search of the Past.* New York: RosettaBooks, 2015.

Kamber, Peter. *Biographie-Projekt Bernhard Falkenberg.* Berlin: Unpublished manuscript, 2012.

Kanc, Shimon, editor. *Yizkor Book for Włodawa and the Sobibor Area.* Tel Aviv: Włodawa Immigrants Association in Israel, 1974.

Lustigman Omelinski, Sara. *In a Land of Forest and Darkness. The Holocaust Story of Two Jewish Partisans.* Oegstgeest: Amsterdam Publishers, 2021.

Myers, Isidore C. *Remember: A Book to Honor the Family I Never Knew.* Newport Beach: 1992.

Silberklang, David. *Gates of Tears: The Holocaust in the Lublin District.* Jerusalem: Yad Vashem Publications, 2013.

Skwirowski, Kryzsztof. *Świat Zapomniany. Historia Żdów Włodawskich 1918–1945 [The World Forgotten: History of the Jews of Włodawa].* Włodawa: Muzeum Pojezierza Łęczyńsko-Włodawskiego, 2014.

Werner, Harold. *Fighting Back. A Memoir of Jewish Resistance in World War II.* New York: Columbia University Press, 1994.

Zamoyska-Panek, Christine. *Have you Forgotten? A Memoir of Poland, 1939–1945.* New York: Doubleday, 1989.

Testimony and Interviews

Garin, Michael. Conversation with Jeannette Grunhaus de Gelman [Recording]. Tel Aviv, October 2000.

Grunhaus Lederman, Alexandra. Conversation with Joseph Gelman [Recording]. Maracaibo, 1993.

– Interview for the USC Shoah Foundations, Survivors of the Shoah: Visual History Archive, no. 13907. Caracas, April 16, 1996.

– Conversation with Jeannette Grunhaus de Gelman. Trip to Poland, September 2000.

Grunhaus, Hil. Statement in letter on events of the war in Włodawa sent to the World Jewish Congress. New York, August 23, 1961.

– Preliminary testimony for the Hanover trial. Germany Embassy in Caracas. July 26, 1964.

– Statement sworn before Notary Erich Müller. Hanover, July 24, 1965.

– Conversation with Joseph Gelman [Recording]. Maracaibo, April 1985.

Omelinski, Sara. Conversations with Leon Grunhaus and Jeannette Grunhaus de Gelman [Recording]. Tel Aviv, 2014–2015.

Rubaka, Pnina. Conversation with Jeannette Grunhaus de Gelman [Recording.] Tel Aviv, October 2000.

Archival Sources

The preliminary statements collected before the Hanover trial (1964) of those responsible for Nazi war crimes in Włodawa has been mainly drawn from Yad Vashem documents. They can also be found in the archives of USHMM and in the Landesarchiv of Hanover.

The Hanover material was primarily used in the preparation of Chapter 13 and the appendix on the trial.

Yad Vashem

Preliminary testimony of some Włodawa survivors prior to the Hanover trial, namely:

Cyn, Josef Dawid

Huberman, Yehezkel

Kachan, Simcha

Knopmacher, Mosze

Knopmacher, Pnina

Lederman, Wigdor

Lederman, Simon

Melcer, Eliezer

Omelinski, Sara

Rotenberg, Aisig

Rotstein, Grete

Rozanka, Samuel (Leib)

Turkienicz, Tamara

All statements from the above are contained in the institution's archive groups: TR.10/1412,TR.10/631.1, TR.10/631.2, TR.10/631, TR.10/M1412.

Other Preliminary Testimony

Falkenberg, Bernhard. Testimony provided during questioning on events in Włodawa between 1940 and 1943, sent by the Hanover Prosecutor's Office on December 1, 1961.

– Testimony at the Bernau District Court, Democratic German Republic. April 19, 1962.

– Testimony at the Bernau District Court, Democratic German Republic. July 16, 1965.

Holtzheimer, Franz. Testimony at the Hanover Regional Court. Hanover, February 2,1962, and January 16, 1963.

Lemberger, Leon. Jewish Historical Institute, Archive ZIH PODPIS (1), #68, Warsaw. September 19, 1947.

Rabinowicz, Motel. Jewish Historical Institute, Archive #49E/2202, Warsaw. Date unknown.

Selinger, Willy, Testimony at the Hanover Regional Court, Hanover. February 21, 1963.

Archives Consulted in Germany

Niedersächsisches Landesarchiv-Hauptstaatsarchiv Hannover.

Archives Nos. 721 Hannover Acc 16/97 Nr. 75/76.

Archives Nos. 721 Hannover Acc 97/97 Nr. 14/1–14/77.

TR. 21/104, Indictment by the Hanover Regional Court. July 24, 1963.

Archive LG Hannover of 29-10-1964, 2Ks 4/63 and BHG Hannover of 7-12-1965, 5StR 411/65. Final Verdict.

Polish Civil Registries

Lublin State Archives, Chelm Office and Włodawa Office.

ABOUT THE AUTHOR

Jeannette Grunhaus de Gelman is a Venezuelan teacher, researcher, and writer. She was born in Szczecin, Poland in 1946, the daughter of Polish survivors who came from Włodawa. That same year, her family emigrated to Venezuela, settling in Maracaibo. Gelman received her undergraduate degree in French from Wellesley College. She went on to receive an MA in Spanish Literature from New York University (Madrid) in 1970 and in 1976 was awarded her MA in the Teaching of French from the Université de Paris III.

She was a professor of French Language and Literature at the Universidad del Zulia in Maracaibo from 1971 to 1996. In 2013 she moved to Miami, Florida.

From 2013 to 2018 she was a Research Scholar at Florida Atlantic University in Boca Raton, focusing on Holocaust studies.

On Sunny Days We Sang was first published in Spanish in 2018 under the title, *En los días claros cantábamos*. It is the author's first full-length work, telling the story of her parents' survival in Nazi-occupied Poland during the Second World War.

Dear Reader,

If you have enjoyed reading my book,
please do leave a review on Amazon or Goodreads. A few kind words
would be enough. This would be greatly appreciated.

Alternatively, if you have read my book as Kindle eBook you could
leave a rating.
That is just one simple click, indicating how many stars of five you
think this book deserves.
This will only cost you a split second.

Thank you very much in advance!

AMSTERDAM PUBLISHERS HOLOCAUST LIBRARY

The series **Holocaust Survivor Memoirs World War II** consists of the following autobiographies of survivors:

Outcry. Holocaust Memoirs, by Manny Steinberg

Hank Brodt Holocaust Memoirs. A Candle and a Promise, by Deborah Donnelly

The Dead Years. Holocaust Memoirs, by Joseph Schupack

Rescued from the Ashes. The Diary of Leokadia Schmidt, Survivor of the Warsaw Ghetto, by Leokadia Schmidt

My Lvov. Holocaust Memoir of a twelve-year-old Girl, by Janina Hescheles

Remembering Ravensbrück. From Holocaust to Healing, by Natalie Hess

Wolf. A Story of Hate, by Zeev Scheinwald with Ella Scheinwald

Save my Children. An Astonishing Tale of Survival and its Unlikely Hero, by Leon Kleiner with Edwin Stepp

Holocaust Memoirs of a Bergen-Belsen Survivor & Classmate of Anne Frank, by Nanette Blitz Konig

Defiant German - Defiant Jew. A Holocaust Memoir from inside the Third Reich, by Walter Leopold with Les Leopold

In a Land of Forest and Darkness. The Holocaust Story of two Jewish Partisans, by Sara Lustigman Omelinski

Holocaust Memories. Annihilation and Survival in Slovakia, by Paul Davidovits

From Auschwitz with Love. The Inspiring Memoir of Two Sisters' Survival, Devotion and Triumph Told by Manci Grunberger Beran & Ruth Grunberger Mermelstein, by Daniel Seymour

Remetz. Resistance Fighter and Survivor of the Warsaw Ghetto, by Jan Yohay Remetz

My March Through Hell. A Young Girl's Terrifying Journey to Survival, by Halina Kleiner with Edwin Stepp

Roman's Journey, by Roman Halter

Rudi Haymann, Beyond Frontiers. My extraordinary decade, 1938–1948, Europe–Africa–America

The Engineer, by Henry Reiss

Memoirs by Elmar Rivosh, Sculptor (1906-1967). Riga Ghetto and Beyond, by Elmar Rivosh

----

The series **Holocaust Survivor True Stories WWII** consists of the following biographies:

Among the Reeds. The true story of how a family survived the Holocaust, by Tammy Bottner

A Holocaust Memoir of Love & Resilience. Mama's Survival from Lithuania to America, by Ettie Zilber

Living among the Dead. My Grandmother's Holocaust Survival Story of Love and Strength, by Adena Bernstein Astrowsky

Heart Songs. A Holocaust Memoir, by Barbara Gilford

Shoes of the Shoah. The Tomorrow of Yesterday, by Dorothy Pierce

Hidden in Berlin. A Holocaust Memoir, by Evelyn Joseph Grossman

Separated Together. The Incredible True WWII Story of Soulmates
Stranded an Ocean Apart, by Kenneth P. Price, Ph.D.

The Man Across the River. The incredible story of one man's will to survive
the Holocaust, by Zvi Wiesenfeld

If Anyone Calls, Tell Them I Died. A Memoir, by Emanuel (Manu) Rosen

The House on Thrömerstrasse. A Story of Rebirth and Renewal in the Wake
of the Holocaust, by Ron Vincent

Dancing with my Father. His hidden past. Her quest for truth. How Nazi
Vienna shaped a family's identity, by Jo Sorochinsky

The Story Keeper. Weaving the Threads of Time and Memory - A Memoir,
by Fred Feldman

Krisia's Silence. The Girl who was not on Schindler's List, by Ronny Hein

Defying Death on the Danube. A Holocaust Survival Story, by Debbie J.
Callahan with Henry Stern

A Doorway to Heroism. A decorated German-Jewish Soldier who became an
American Hero, by Rabbi W. Jack Romberg

The Shoemaker's Son. The Life of a Holocaust Resister, by Laura Beth Bakst

The Redhead of Auschwitz. A True Story, by Nechama Birnbaum

Land of Many Bridges. My Father's Story, by Bela Ruth Samuel Tenenholtz

Creating Beauty from the Abyss. The Amazing Story of Sam Herciger, Auschwitz Survivor and Artist, by Lesley Ann Richardson

On Sunny Days We Sang. A Holocaust Story of Survival and Resilience, by Jeannette Grunhaus de Gelman

Painful Joy. A Holocaust Family Memoir, by Max J. Friedman

I Give You My Heart. A True Story of Courage and Survival, by Wendy Holden

In the Time of Madmen, by Mark A. Prelas

Monsters and Miracles. Horror, Heroes and the Holocaust, by Ira Wesley Kitmacher

Flower of Vlora. Growing up Jewish in Communist Albania, by Anna Kohen

Aftermath: Coming of Age on Three Continents. A Memoir, by Annette Libeskind Berkovits

Not a real Enemy. The True Story of a Hungarian Jewish Man's Fight for Freedom, by Robert Wolf

Zaidy's War. Four Armies, Three Continents, Two Brothers. One Man's Impossible Story of Endurance, by Martin Bodek

The Glassmaker's Son. Looking for the World my Father left behind in Nazi Germany, by Peter Kupfer

The Apprentice of Buchenwald. The True Story of the Teenage Boy Who Sabotaged Hitler's War Machine, by Oren Schneider

Good for a Single Journey, by Helen Joyce

Burying the Ghosts. She escaped Nazi Germany only to have her life torn apart by the woman she saved from the camps: her mother, by Sonia Case

American Wolf. From Nazi Refugee to American Spy. A True Story, by Audrey Birnbaum

Bipolar Refugee. A Saga of Survival and Resilience, by Peter Wiesner

Before the Beginning and After the End, by Hymie Anisman

The series **Jewish Children in the Holocaust** consists of the following autobiographies of Jewish children hidden during WWII in the Netherlands:

Searching for Home. The Impact of WWII on a Hidden Child, by Joseph Gosler

See You Tonight and Promise to be a Good Boy! War memories, by Salo Muller

Sounds from Silence. Reflections of a Child Holocaust Survivor, Psychiatrist and Teacher, by Robert Krell

Sabine's Odyssey. A Hidden Child and her Dutch Rescuers, by Agnes Schipper

The Journey of a Hidden Child, by Harry Pila and Robin Black

The series **New Jewish Fiction** consists of the following novels, written by Jewish authors. All novels are set in the time during or after the Holocaust.

The Corset Maker. A Novel, by Annette Libeskind Berkovits

Escaping the Whale. The Holocaust is over. But is it ever over for the next generation? by Ruth Rotkowitz

When the Music Stopped. Willy Rosen's Holocaust, by Casey Hayes

Hands of Gold. One Man's Quest to Find the Silver Lining in Misfortune, by Roni Robbins

The Girl Who Counted Numbers. A Novel, by Roslyn Bernstein

There was a garden in Nuremberg. A Novel, by Navina Michal Clemerson

The Butterfly and the Axe, by Omer Bartov

To Live Another Day. A Novel, Elizabeth Rosenberg

A Worthy Life. Based on a True Story, by Dahlia Moore

———

The series **Holocaust Heritage** consists of the following memoirs by 2G:

The Cello Still Sings. A Generational Story of the Holocaust and of the Transformative Power of Music, by Janet Horvath

The Fire and the Bonfire. A Journey into Memory, by Ardyn Halter

The Silk Factory: Finding Threads of My Family's True Holocaust Story, by Michael Hickins

———

The series **Holocaust Books for Young Adults** consists of the following novels, based on true stories:

The Boy behind the Door. How Salomon Kool Escaped the Nazis. Inspired by a True Story, by David Tabatsky

Running for Shelter. A True Story, by Suzette Sheft

The Precious Few. An Inspirational Saga of Courage based on True Stories, by David Twain with Art Twain

---

The series **WW2 Historical Fiction** consists of the following novels, some of which are based on true stories:

Mendelevski's Box. A Heartwarming and Heartbreaking Jewish Survivor's Story, by Roger Swindells

A Quiet Genocide. The Untold Holocaust of Disabled Children WW2 Germany, by Glenn Bryant

The Knife-Edge Path, by Patrick T. Leahy

Brave Face. The Inspiring WWII Memoir of a Dutch/German Child, by I. Caroline Crocker and Meta A. Evenbly

When We Had Wings. The Gripping Story of an Orphan in Janusz Korczak's Orphanage. A Historical Novel, by Tami Shem-Tov

Jacob's Courage. Romance and Survival amidst the Horrors of War, by Charles S. Weinblatt

Want to be an AP book reviewer?

Reviews are very important in a world dominated by the social media and social proof.

Please drop us a line if you want to join the *AP review team* and show us at least one review already posted on Amazon for one of our books.

info@amsterdampublishers.com